BRANCH LINES TO SUDBURY

Vic Mitchell

Vic Mitchell

MP Middleton Press

Front cover: With its train at the sharply curved platform at Sudbury, class D16/3 4-4-0 no. 62574 waits to leave for Colchester, sometime in 1954. (G.W.Powell/Colour-Rail.com)

Back cover lower: Waiting at Haverhill is the answer to economical railway operation - a railbus. It is German-built no. E79961. (Colour-Rail.com)

Back cover upper: Running into the branch platform at Marks Tey on 20th May 1961 is a smart class 105 DMU. The road bridge has been raised in readiness for electrification of the main line. (Colour-Rail.com)

Published May 2012

ISBN 978 1 908174 19 2

Design Deborah Esher

Published by
Middleton Press
Easebourne Lane
Midhurst
West Sussex
GU29 9AZ
Tel: 01730 813169
Fax: 01730 812601
Email: info@middletonpress.co.uk
www.middletonpress.co.uk

Printed in the United Kingdom by Henry Ling Limited, at the Dorset Press, Dorchester, DT1 1HD

CONTENTS

INDEX

ACKNOWLEDGEMENTS

I am very grateful for the assistance received from many of those mentioned in the credits, also to A.R.Carder, G.Croughton, G.Kenworthy, G.Gull, S.C.Jenkins, N.Langridge, B.Lewis, Mr D. and Dr S.Salter and, in particular my wife, who has meticulously typeset my scribblings over 30 years. Included in my appreciation is Chris Cock, who has kindly supplied data from the Bryan Wilson Signalling Register.

I. The routes are shown as in about 1900, with the lines of this album in black. Railway heritage sites were established at Chappel & Wakes Colne and also at Sible & Castle Hedingham. (Railway Magazine)

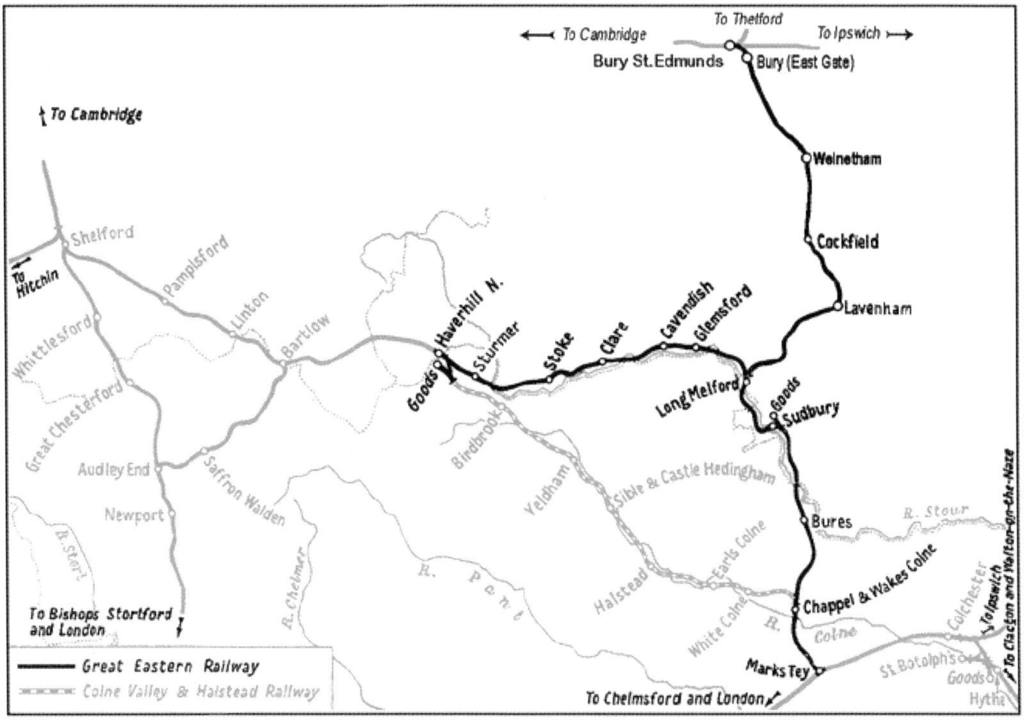

GEOGRAPHICAL SETTINGS

We will look at the routes from north to south. The old market town of Bury St. Edmunds is only a few miles north of the source of the River Lark, which flows close to the centre of the urban area and a little to the east of the station. The route south was over chalk upland as far south as Sudbury.

The line east from Haverhill was over similar agricultural terrain and from Sturmer was in the valley of the east flowing River Stour. It turns south at Sudbury, where it leaves the chalk in favour of clay. The railway followed this waterway as far as Bures, where the Stour turns east again to enter the sea at Harwich.

The route south to Marks Tey is undulating, the line crossing the east flowing River Colne on a viaduct at Chappel and the small Roman River on its approach to Marks Tey.

The county boundary between Suffolk and Essex was close to the route between Haverhill and Bures, the latter being south of it. The Stour Navigation once provided local transport with small boats between Manningtree and Sudbury.

The maps are to the scale of 25ins to 1 mile, with north at the top, unless otherwise indicated.

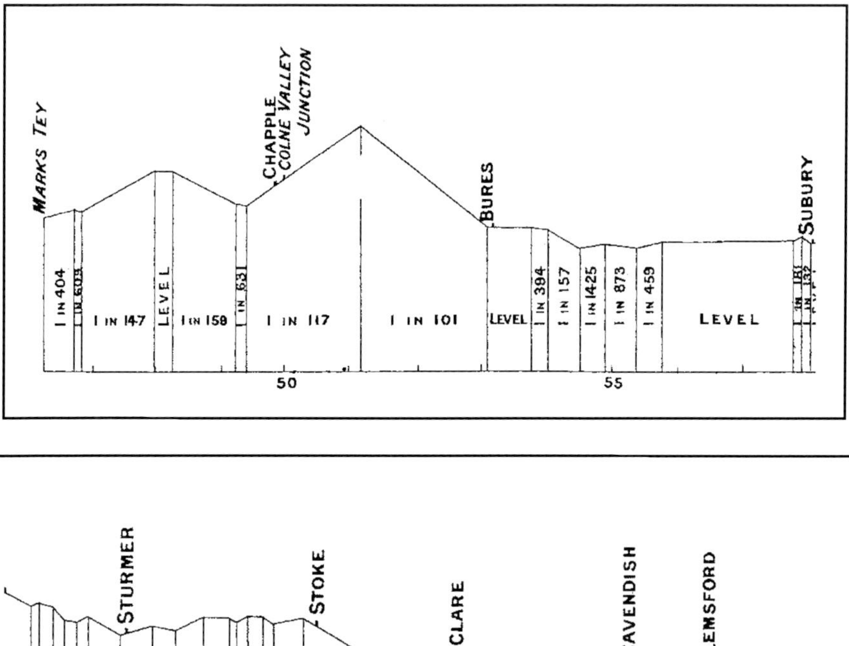

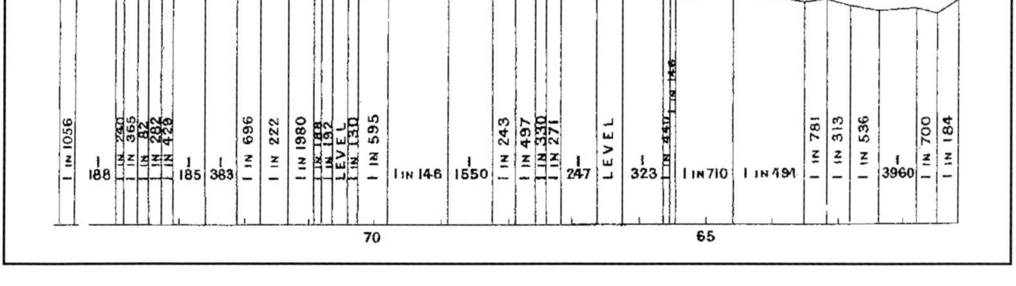

HISTORICAL BACKGROUND

The line between Brentwood and Colchester was opened by the Eastern Counties Railway in 1843. The Ipswich and Bury St. Edmunds section was completed by a company of that name in 1846 and it became part of the Eastern Union Railway in the following year. Both operators were constituents of the Great Eastern Railway from 1862.

The Colchester, Stour Valley, Sudbury & Halstead Railway received its Act on 26th June 1846 and opened only the part between Marks Tey and Sudbury on 2nd July 1849. The company was leased to the EUR in 1849, it having operated all trains from the outset. The line became GER property in 1898.

The Colne Valley & Halstead Railway was incorporated on 30th June 1856 and it opened between Chappel and Halstead on 16th April 1860. It reached Yeldham on 26th May 1862 and was extended to Haverhill on 10th May 1863.

A GER Act of 7th August 1862 was for the building of a line from Shelford (south of Cambridge) to Sudbury via Haverhill, Clare and Long Melford. It opened between Shelford and Haverhill on 1st June 1865. There was a goods connection between the two lines at Haverhill. It carried regular passenger trains later.

The Haverhill to Sudbury and the Bury St. Edmunds to Long Melford sections both came into use on 9th August 1865.

Bury St. Edmunds received a line from Newmarket in 1854 and one from Thetford in 1876, the latter lasting until 1960.

The GER became part of the London & North Eastern Railway in 1923 and this formed much of the Eastern Region of British Railways upon nationalisation in 1948.

Passenger service was withdrawn between Bury St. Edmunds and Long Melford on 1st April 1961, between Haverhill, Halstead and Chappel & Wakes Colne on 1st January 1962 and between Shelford, Long Melford and Sudbury on 6th March 1967. Only the Marks Tey to Sudbury section remained open subsequently. The dates of withdrawal of goods services, are given in the captions.

The line became part of Network SouthEast on 10th June 1986. Privatisation resulted in the route being branded First Great Eastern on 5th January 1997 when FirstBus was awarded a 7¼ year franchise. This became First Group, but the operation was transferred to National Express, which applied the meaningless name of 'one' from 1st April 2004. It was rebranded National Express East Anglia in 2008. The franchise moved to Abellio, a Dutch state railway subsidiary, on 5th February 2012. Its duration was 29 months and the name used was Abellio Greater Anglia.

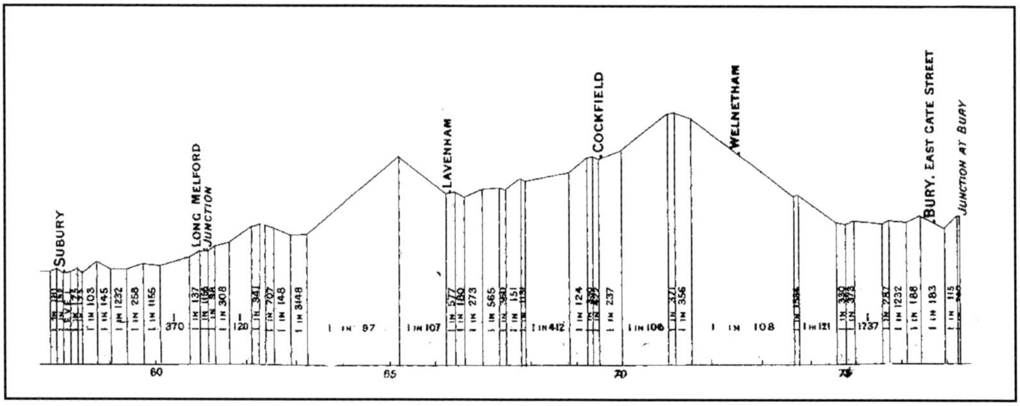

PASSENGER SERVICES

The tables below are to give an indication of the basic train frequencies on the three routes and exclude trains running on less than five days per week and also through trains between the Midlands and coastal resorts, which often ran in the Summer.

Marks Tey to Sudbury

	Weekdays	Sundays
1869	4	2
1880	6	2
1895	7	3
1915	10	4
1930	8	3
1945	6	3
1960	7	5
1985	10	4
2012	18	15

Haverhill eastwards

	Weekdays	Sundays
1869	3	0
1880	3	2
1895	5	0
1915	7	2
1930	5	0
1945	5	0
1960	6	0

Bury St. Edmunds southwards

	Weekdays	Sundays
1869	3	0
1880	5	0
1895	6	0
1915	7	0
1930	6	0
1945	5	0
1960	4	0

Colne Valley services will appear in a future album. The origins and destinations of trains has varied greatly over the years and many examples are given in the captions.

June 1869

CAMBRIDGE, HAVERHILL, BURY, SUDBURY, MARK'S TEY, & COLCHESTER.—Great Eastern.

Miles from Cambridg.	Fares fm London 1 cl. s. d.	2 cl. s. d.	3 cl. s. d.	gov s. d.	From Oxford, Bedford, &c., 120.	Week Days. 1,2,3 gov	1&2 mrn	1&2 mrn	1,2,3 aft	1,2,3 aft	Sndys. 1,2,3 gov	1,2,3 aft
	....	....	....	....	Bishopsgate Sta., LONDON 88 dp		6 20	11 0	....	5b0		
	....	....	....	....	**Cambridge** ..dep		9 45	2 0	....	7 10		
3½	11 0	8 9	5 6	4 6	Shelford		9 52	2 8	....	7 18		
7½	12 0	9 9	7 3	4 10½	Abington		a	2 17	....	7 26		
10½	12 6	10 0	7 6	5 1	Linton		10 9	2 26	....	7 34		
12¼	13 0	10 6	7 9	5 3	Bartlow 89		1015	2 33	....	7 41		
18¼	13 9	10 8	8 1	5 9	**Haverhill** (see be-	gov.	1030	2 50	....	7 56		
20¼	14 9	11 9	8 9	5 11	Sturmer .. [low)		a	2 57	....	8 2		
23	14 6	11 6	8 9	5 9½	Stoke		a	3 6	....	8 10		
25½	14 0	11 3	8 6	5 7½	Clare		1048	3 14	....	8 17		
27¾	13 6	10 9	8 0	5 4½	Cavendish		1055	3 22	....	8 25		
29	13 2	10 6	7 11	5 3½	Glemsford		11 1	3 26	....	8 30		
31½	12 6	10 0	7 6	5 1	**Melford** ....arr		11 7	3 33	....	8 37		
	16 0	12 9	9 6	6 5	48½ **Bury** ....dep	7 35	....	3 20	5 0	....		
	16 0	12 9	9 6	6 5	47½ **Bury** (E.G.St)	7 38	....	3 23	5 5	....		
	15 0	12 0	9 0	6 0½	41½ Welnetham..	a	....	a	a	....		
	13 9	11 0	8 3	5 6	37 Lavenham ..	8 2	....	3 47	5 45	....		
	....	....	....	....	— Melford..arr	8 14	....	4 0	6 0	....		
—	....	....	....	....	**Melford** ....dep	8 15	1115	4 1	6 5	8 47		
34½	12 0	9 6	7 3	4 10	**Sudbury** .. arr	8 22	1125	4 8	6 15	8 55		
					Sudbury .. dep	8 25	1140	4 12	6 30	....	8 55	4 5
39½	11 0	8 9	6 6	4 5	Bures	a	a	a	a	....	9 5	4 15
43	10 3	8 3	6 3	4 1½	Chappel, *see below*	8 47	12 5	4 33	6 51	....	9 17	4 30
46½	9 6	7 6	5 9	3 10	Mark's Tey J. 85	8 57	1215	4 43	7 0	....	9 28	4 45
92¾	....	....	....	....	85 LONDON ..arr	10¾c	4 10	6 35	8 55	....	1215	7 15
51½	10 6	8 6	6 3	4 3	Colchester 82 ar	10 4	1230	4 55	7 35	....	9 50	5 3

b Express from London. c 1&2 exp.; 3rd cl. & Gov. Passengers arrive at 12 10 aft.

e 1&2 exp.; 3rd class and Gov. Passengers arrive at 12 50 aft.

Frm Yarmouth, Norwich, Ipswch, &c., see page 84.	Week Days. 1,2,3 gov	1,2,3 mrn	1&2 aft	1&2 exp	1&2 aft	1,2,3 aft	Sndys. 1,2,3 gov	1,2,3 aft
Colchester..dep	....	9 25	1 0	....	5 25	6 52	9 35	4 45
82 L'DON (Bish.)	dep.	7 15	1142	4 25	3 10	5 30	7 15	2 45
Mark's Tey	....	10 0	1 25		5 55	7 30	9 50	5 5
Chappel *see below*	....	1012	1 36		6 6	7 43	10 1	5 18
Bures	....	1022	a	1,2,3	a	a	1011	5 30
Sudbury.. arr	....	1035	2 0	aft	6 28	8 10	1025	5 45
Sudbury.. dep	7 30	1055	2 5	4 20	6 32	....		
Melford ....arr	7 37	11 5	2 13	4 27	6 39	....		
Melford ..dep	....	1113	2 18	....	6 41	....		
Lavenham....	....	1130	2 35	....	6 55	....		
Welnetham ..	....	a	a	....	a	....		
Bury (E.G. St.)	....	12 5	3 5	....	7 21	....		
Bury 84 ..arr	....	1210	3 10	....	7 25	....		
Melford ....dep	7 38	1125	....	4 28	....	....		
Glemsford......	7 45	1131	....	4 34	....	....		
Cavendish	7 49	1135	....	4 38	....	....		
Clare	7 57	1142	....	4 45	....	....		
Stoke	8 4	1149	....	4 52	....	....		
Sturmer [*below*)	8 13	1156	....	4 59	....	....		
Haverhill (*see*	8 21	12 5	....	5 8	....	....		
Bartlow 89	8 36	1218	....	5 21	....	....		
Linton	8 43	1223	....	5 26	....	....		
Abington ..[161	8 52	1229	....	5 32	....	....		
Shelford 89 [101	9 2	1239	....	5 43	....	....		
Cmbdge 88, 93,	9 12	1250	....	5 55	....	....		
89 LONDON ..arr	11e0	3 40	....	9 25	....	....		

a The Trains will ONLY call when required to take up, or set down on informing the Guard at the preceding *stopping* Station.

December 1895

Great Eastern and Colne Valley.

Up.	Week Days.											Sundays.		
	mrn	mrn	mrn	mrn	mrn	mrn	aft	aft	aft	aft	aft	mrn	aft	aft
177 Dereham.dep.	....	....	....	7c40	....	1016	....	....	....	1 45	4 47	....	....	....
Lynn 176 „	....	....	....	8c13	....	9d10	....	1230	....	3 10	5 43	....	....	....
Swaffham....dep.	7 32	....	....	8c44	....	1052	....	1 20	....	4 30	6 50	....	....	....
Holme Hale......	7 41	....	....	8c53	....	11 1	....	1 29	....	4 39	6 59	....	....	....
Watton	7 53	....	....	9 5	....	1113	....	1 40	....	4 51	7 11	....	....	....
Stow Bedon..[ham	8 0	....	....	9 12	....	1120	....		....	4 58	7 18	....	....	....
Wretham & Hock-	8 8	....	....	9 20	....	1128	....		....	5 6	7 26	....	....	....
Roudham Jn { arr.	....	....	....	9 26	....	....	....		....	....	....	....	....	....
170, 171 { dep.	....	....	....	9 28	....	....	....		....	....	....	....	....	....
Thetford 171 arr.	8 21	....	....	9 36	....	1142	....		....	5 20	7 39	....	....	....
170 Norwich { ar		....	....	1035	....	1258	....	Wednesdays only.	....	6 35	8 50	....	....	....
(Thorpe) 171 { dp		....	....	8 35	....	11 8	....		....	4 40	....	....	....	....
Thetford .....dep.		....	....	9 57	....	1217	....		....	5 57	7 53	....	....	....
Thetford Bridge..		....	....	10 1	....	1221	....		....	6 1	7 57	....	....	....
Barnham		....	....	10 7	....	1227	....		....	6 7	8 8	....	....	....
Ingham ......[179		....	....	1018	....	1238	....		....	6 18	8 14	....	....	....
Bury St. Edmunds	Mondays only.	....	....	1025	....	1245	....		....	6 25	8 21	....	....	....
186 Ipswich.. arr.		....	....	1153	....	3 52	....		....	7 50	9 24	....	....	....
179 Cambridge „		....	....	1 5	....	4 33	....		....	....	....	....	....	....
Bury St. Edmunds		7 30	9 25	1110	Fridays only.	2 35	4 5	....	5 42	....	Stop	....	....	....
Bury (East Gate)..		7 33	9 28	1114		2 39	4 8	....	5 45	....	....	....	....	....
Welnetham.......		7 41	9 36	1122		2 47	4 16	....	5 54	....	....	....	....	....
Cockfield		7 46	9 41	1128		2 53	4 22	....	6 0	....	....	....	....	....
Lavenham		7 53	9 48	1135		3 0	4 29	....	6 7	....	....	....	....	....
Long Melford arr.		8 3	9 58	1145		3 10	4 39	aft	6 18	....	aft	....	....	....
Melford and Cambridge Branch.														
Cambridge d	....	....	9 0	1040		1 45	....	4 46	....	....	7 10	....	....	....
170 London*d	....	....	5 45	8 45		1155	....	2 30	....	....	5 15	....	....	....
Shelford	....	....	9 7	1048		1 52	....	4 53	....	....	7 18	....	....	....
Pampisford ..	....	....	9 15	1058		2 0	....	5 1	....	....	7 26	....	....	....
Linton	....	....	9 22	11 4		2 8	....	5 8	....	....	7 34	....	....	....
170 London*d		....	5 45	....	1030	....	....	2b50	....	....	5 15	....	....	....
Bartlow 172.		....	9 28	11 9	1 0	2 14	....	5 14	....	....	7 40	....	....	....
Haverhill....		....	9 43	1122	1 12	2 29	....	5 28	....	....	7 55	....	....	....
Sturmer		....	9 49	1127	....	2 34	....	5 33	....	....	8 0	....	....	....
Stoke........	Mondays only.	....	9 55	1133	....	2 40	....	5 39	....	....	8 6	....	....	....
Clare ‡		....	10 2	1139	....	2 46	....	5 45	....	....	8 13	....	....	....
Cavendish ...		....	1010	1145	....	2 52	....	5 51	....	....	8 19	....	....	....
Glemsford ...		....	1014	1149	....	2 56	....	5 55	....	....	8 24	....	....	....
Long Melford		....	1019	1154	....	3 1	....	6 0	....	....	8 29	....	....	....
Long Melford dep.		8 5	1021	1159	....	3 14	4 44	6 2	6 20	....	8 31	....	....	....
Sudbury .. { arr.		8 11	1027	12 5	....	3 20	4 50	6 8	6 26	....	8 37	....	....	....
Sudbury .. { dep.		8 13	1029	12 8	....	3 22	4 52		6 30	....	8 39	9 20	4 25	5 50
Bures		8 22	1038	1217	....	3 31	5 1	....	6 39	....	8 48	9 29	4 34	5 59
Chappel ......arr.	mrn	8 30	1046	1225	....	3 39	5 9	....	6 47	....	8 56	9 37	4 42	6 7
Colne Valley and Halstead														
Haverhill dp.	7 40	....	9 55	....	....	2 50	....	....	5 50	....	....	8 45	3 40	....
Birdbrook....	7 49	....	10 3	....	....	2 59	....	....	5 59	....	....	8 54	3 50	....
Yeldham	7 57	....	1014	....	....	3 8	....	....	6 9	....	....	9 4	4 0	....
Hedingham †	8 3	....	1021	....	....	3 14	....	....	6 17	....	....	9 12	4 10	....
Halstead......	8 12	....	1031	....	....	3 22	....	....	6 26	....	....	9 21	4 22	5 50
Colne.........	8 17	....	1036	....	....	3 27	....	....	6 31	....	....	9 26	4 27	5 56
Chappel. arr.	8 28	....	1045	....	....	3 37	....	....	6 40	....	....	9 35	4 37	6 6
Chappel......dep.		8 34	1050	1227	....	3 42	5 11	....	6 51	....	9 0	9 41	4 46	6 11
Mark's Tey 185..	....	8 41	1058	1235	....	3 50	5 18	....	6 59	....	9 7	9 49	4 54	6 19
185 London * arr.	....	1010	1220	2 10	....	5 50	7e33	....	8 52	....	....	1220	....	7 50
Colchester 191 arr	....	9 12	1110	1252	....	4 5	5 31	....	7 15	....	9 17	10 5	5 14	....
182 Ipswich.. arr.	....	9 58	1152	1 53	....	4 45	6 17	....	9 5	....	1024	1048	5 54	....

October 1945

MARK'S TEY, SUDBURY, BURY ST. EDMUNDS, HAVERHILL (North)

Miles		Week Days											Sundays				
		mrn	mrn	mrn	mrn	mrn	aft	aft S	aft	aft	aft	aft	mrn	mrn	aft	aft	aft
	3 London (L'poolSt) dep	..	..	8 50	10 0	..	1 0	2 10	2 30	4 54	..	7 30	8 30	..	5 0	..	7 30
	3 Colchester ..... „	..	..	8 57	11 2	..	2 0	3 25	4 0	6 16	..	9 0	9 56	..	5 57	..	9 0
—	Mark's Tey......... dep	..	..	9 15	1135	1143	2 29	3 48	4 18	6 35	6K44	9 13	1025	1036	6 30	6 41	9 15
3½	Chappel & Wakes Colne.	..	..	9 25	1143	1150	2 37	3 57	4 27	6 43	6K51	9 22	1035	1043	6 40	6 48	9 24
6¾	Bures	..	..	9 34	1152	To Haverhill (Table 18)	2 46	4 6	4 36	6 52	To Haverhill (Table 18)	9 31	1044	To Haverhill (Table 18)	6 49	To Haverhill (Table 18)	9 33
11¾	Sudbury (Suffolk). { arr	..	..	9 42	12 0		2 54	4 15	4 44	7 0		9 39	1052		6 57		9 41
	Sudbury (Suffolk). { dep	6 35	7 55	9 55	12 9		2 58	Third class only	5 5	7 6		9 41	..		7 0		..
14½	Long Melford....... arr	6 41	8 1	10 1	1215		3 4		5 11	7 12		9 47	..		7 6		..
—	Long Melford..... dep	..	8 6	1024	1228		3 15		..	7 14		..	..		..		..
20	Lavenham	..	8 20	1036	1240		3 26		..	7 27		..	..		..		..
23½	Cockfield (Suffolk)....	..	8 30	1044	1248		3 33		..	7 38		..	..		..		..
26½	Welnetham	..	8 36	1051	1255		3 39		..	7 46		..	..		..		..
31½	Bury St. Edmunds arr	..	8 48	11 0	1 4		3 50		..	8 0		..	..		..		..
—	Long Melford ...... dep	6 43	..	10 6	1218	..	3 7	..	5 19	..	..	..	..	..	..	..	..
17½	Glemsford	6 48	..	1011	1223	..	3 12	..	5 24	..	..	..	..	..	..	..	..
18¾	Cavendish	6 52	..	1017	1230	..	3 16	..	5 28	..	..	..	..	..	..	..	..
21¼	Clare....................	6 59	..	1025	1236	..	3 22	..	5 34	..	..	..	..	..	..	..	..
23¾	Stoke (Suffolk)..........	7 4	..	1030	1241	..	3 27	..	5 39	..	..	..	..	..	..	..	..
26¼	Sturmer.................	7 10	..	1036	1247	..	3 33	..	5 45	..	..	..	..	..	..	..	..
28¾	Haverhill (North).......	7 19	..	1044	1257	..	3 40	..	5 56	..	..	..	..	..	..	..	..
34½	Bartlow .... arr	7 29	..	1054	1 7	..	3 50	..	6 6	..	..	..	..	..	..	..	..
88½	31 London (L'poolSt) arr	9 53	..	2 4	5R5	..	..	..	..	..	..	..	..	..	..	..	..
—	Bartlow .... dep	7 31	..	1057	1 10	..	3 52	..	6 9	..	..	..	..	..	..	..	..
36½	Linton..................	7 37	..	11 2	1 15	..	3 57	..	6 13	..	..	..	..	..	..	..	..
39	Pampisford..............	7 43	..	11 9	1 21	..	4 3	..	6 19	..	..	..	..	..	..	..	..
43½	Shelford................	7 51	..	1117	1F37	..	4 11	..	6 27	..	..	..	..	..	..	..	..
46½	Cambridge......... arr	8 0	..	1129	1 52	..	4 19	..	6 39	..	..	..	..	..	..	..	..
99	4 London (L'poolSt) arr	9X53	..	2 4	5R5	..	6 48	..	8 50	..	..	..	..	..	..	..	..

A Via Colchester
E or E Except Saturdays
F Arr 1 30 aft
H Arr 5 mins. earlier
K 8 mins. later on Sats.
L Arrive 9 20 mrn
N Arr 3 6 aft on Sats
P Passengers can arrive 4 52 aft on Saturdays, third class only
R Arr 5 10 aft on Sats
S Saturdays only
U Dep 3 50 aft on Sats
X Passengers can arrive 9E48 mrn via Shelford

1. Marks Tey to Bures

MARKS TEY

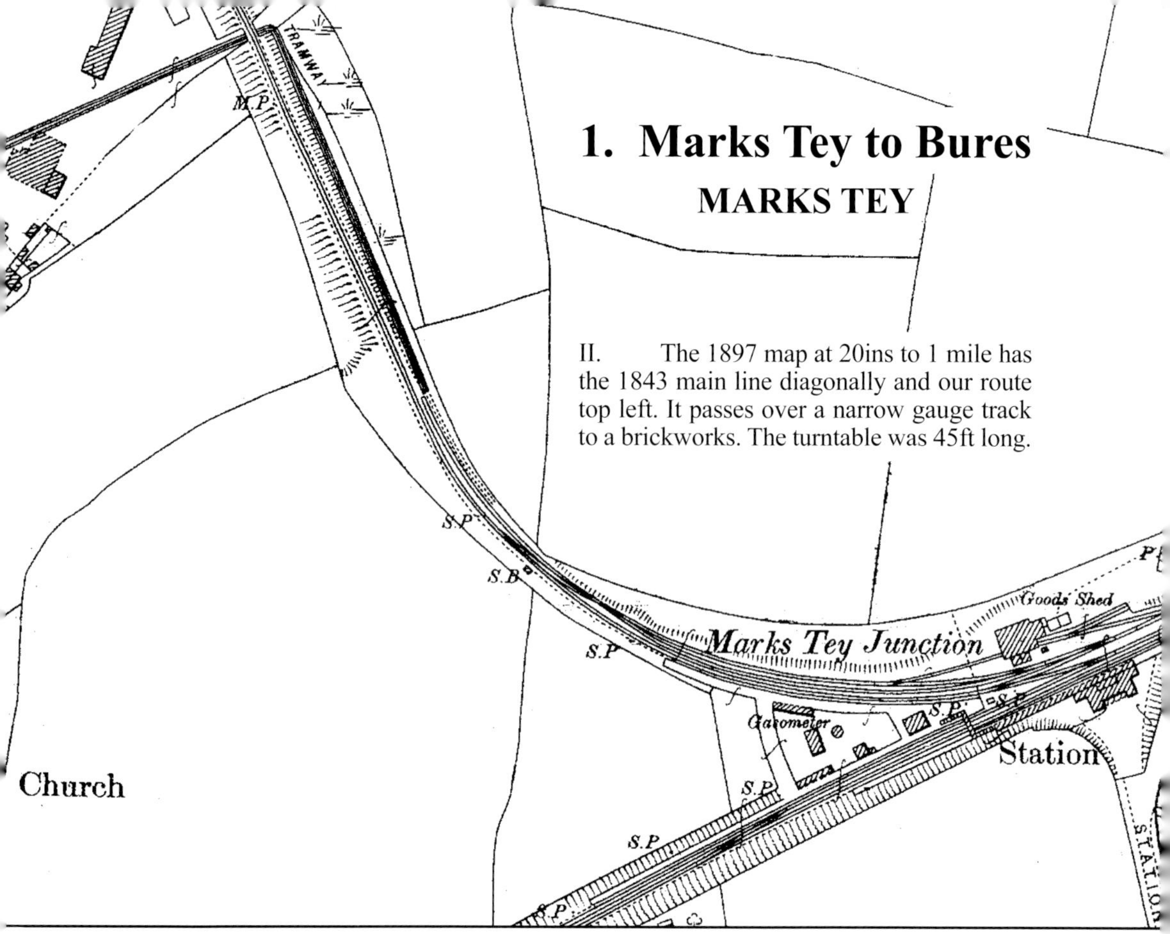

II. The 1897 map at 20ins to 1 mile has the 1843 main line diagonally and our route top left. It passes over a narrow gauge track to a brickworks. The turntable was 45ft long.

1. This northward view along the station approach has the station in the distance. It opened in December 1844 and carried the suffix JUNCTION from 1849 to 1889. (P.Laming coll.)

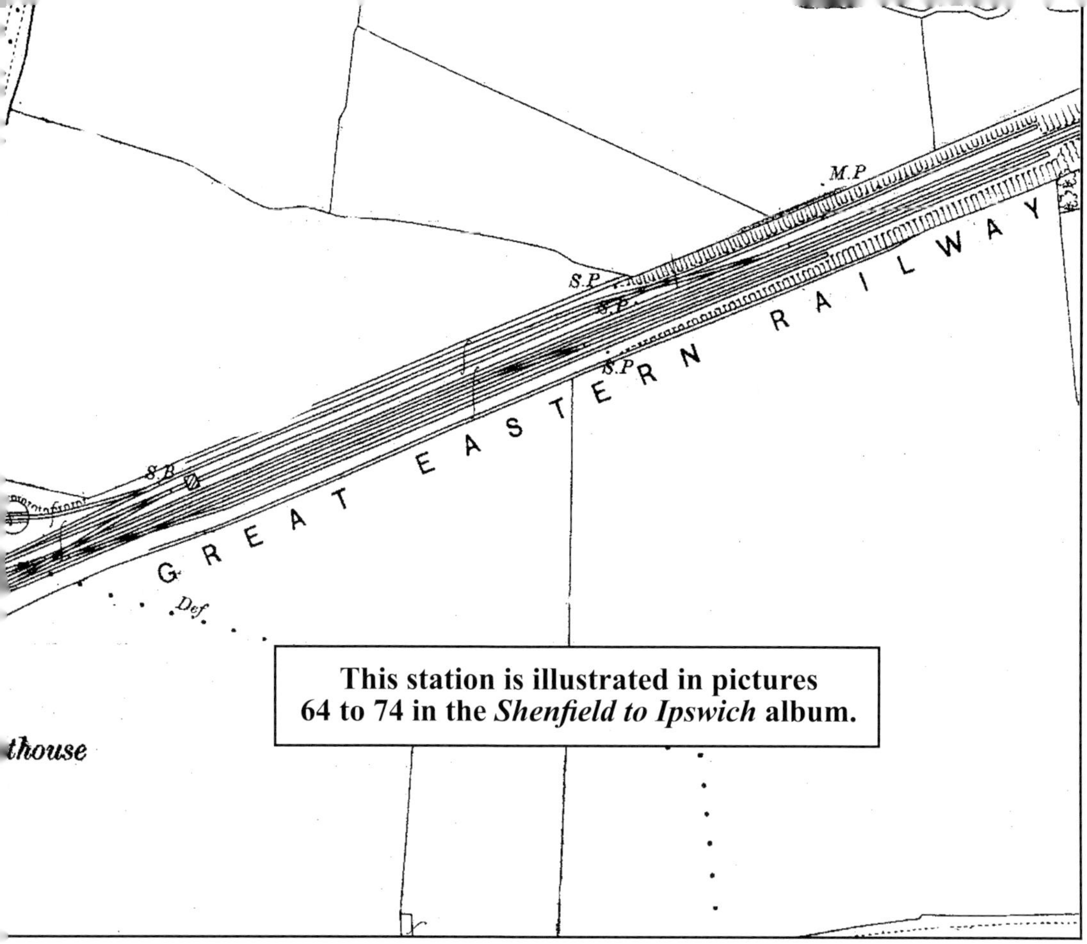

This station is illustrated in pictures 64 to 74 in the *Shenfield to Ipswich* album.

2. Another early postcard and this has the Sudbury line curving to the right. Most trains from it in that era ran to Colchester, with a few continuing to Harwich or Clacton-on-Sea. (P.Laming coll.)

3. We are at the London end of the down platform and the road bridge is just visible, beyond the footbridge. A strange feature of this important junction is that only one of the three platforms was provided with weather protection to its edges. (Dr J.Westhall/A.Vaughan coll.)

4. The curved branch platform is seen on 19th October 1935, when it was occupied by a Cambridge train, hauled by LNER class D15/2 no. 8867. The connection on the left is the northern access to the goods yard. (H.C.Casserley)

5. Class J15 0-6-0 no. 65456 waits to leave with the 12 noon departure for Haverhill via the Colne Valley on 6th April 1955. Five of this class were fitted with tender cabs for use on this route. (R.M.Casserley)

6. In the goods yard on 26th May 1956 is 2-6-0 no. 46468. Freight traffic ceased here in November 1963. A similar view in picture 66 in the companion album shows a Stour Valley train standing at the platform, with a Colne Valley one touching its rear buffers. It would enter as soon as the first one had left, a regular routine. (H.C.Casserley)

7. The signal box was east of the road bridge and this frame was in use until the box closed on 18th October 1997. There were two boxes until 1926; both show on the map as S.B. (D.A.Pollock)

8. It is 4th April 1961 and no. D5537 is at the head of the last train from Bury St. Edmunds, a special. Similar long trains had earlier run from the Midlands and were often destined for Clacton. Electrification of the Chelmsford to Colchester section was completed on 18th June 1962, which is probably the reason for the complex concrete creations crowding the yard. (B.Pask)

9. The goods yard became a car park, as can be seen in this photograph from 15th June 1988, which also includes evidence of electrification and the belated PA system. DMUs had been introduced to the route on 1st January 1959. The platform was cut back to take only two coaches. Completely new up side buildings were opened in January 2012. (P.Hurst/Colour-Rail.com)

SOUTH OF CHAPPEL & WAKES COLNE

10. Chappel Viaduct has 32 arches of 30ft span each, the tallest one being 75ft high. Remedial work was in progress on 16th August 1986 and special arrangements had to be made for the welfare of a group of rare newts resident in its vicinity. (Dr I.C.Scotchman)

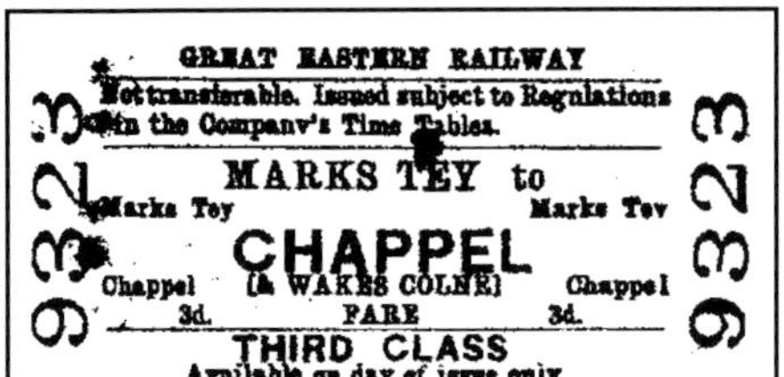

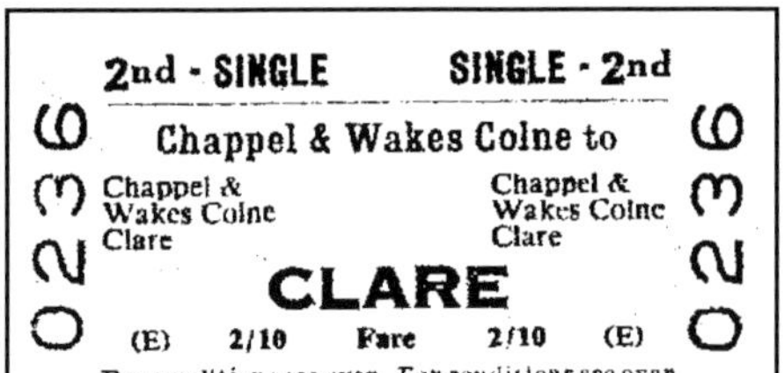

CHAPPEL & WAKES COLNE

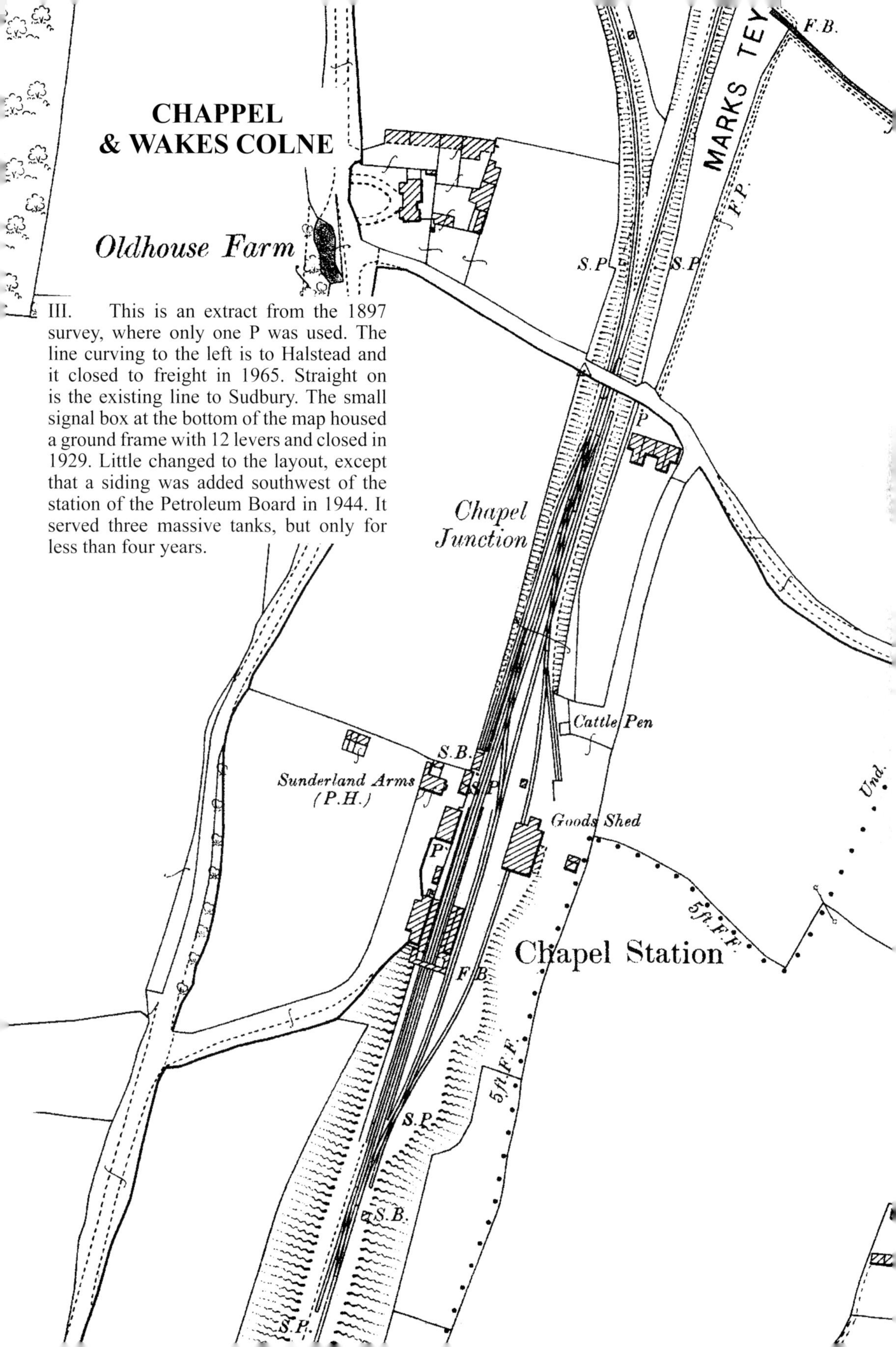

III. This is an extract from the 1897 survey, where only one P was used. The line curving to the left is to Halstead and it closed to freight in 1965. Straight on is the existing line to Sudbury. The small signal box at the bottom of the map housed a ground frame with 12 levers and closed in 1929. Little changed to the layout, except that a siding was added southwest of the station of the Petroleum Board in 1944. It served three massive tanks, but only for less than four years.

11. A fine new building was completed in 1890 and was the subject for a postcard soon afterwards. Secure storage for parcel traffic was provided at road level. (Dr I.C.Scotchman coll.)

12. The 1890 rebuilding included provision of a covered footbridge and generous accommodation on the southbound platform. The population of Wakes Colne fell from 480 in 1901 to 435 in 1961; Chappel had even fewer. (P.Laming coll.)

13. Class J15 0-6-0 no. 65477 enters from the north and passes the permanent way hut and trolley. The first of this class of locomotive was completed by the GER in 1883. (Dr I.C.Scotchman)

14. Class E4 2-4-0 no. 62784 was built in 1894 and runs in with the 11.5am Cambridge to Colchester stopping train on 27th November 1954. The loading gauge is profiled against the sky. Colne and Stour Valley trains were divided and joined here until that era. (P.J.Kelley)

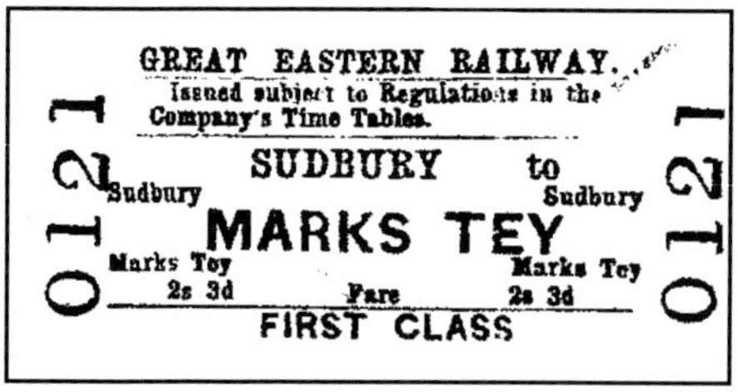

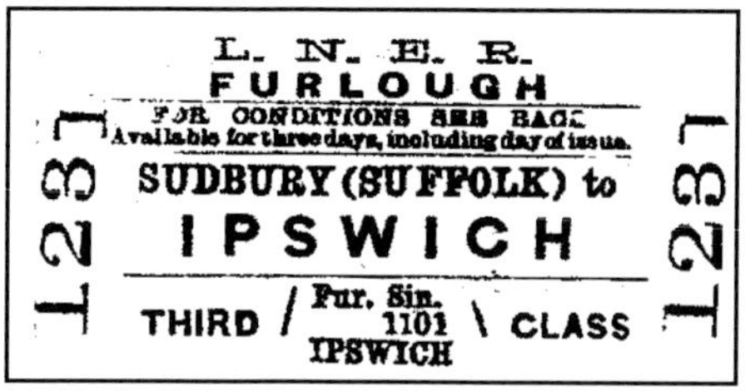

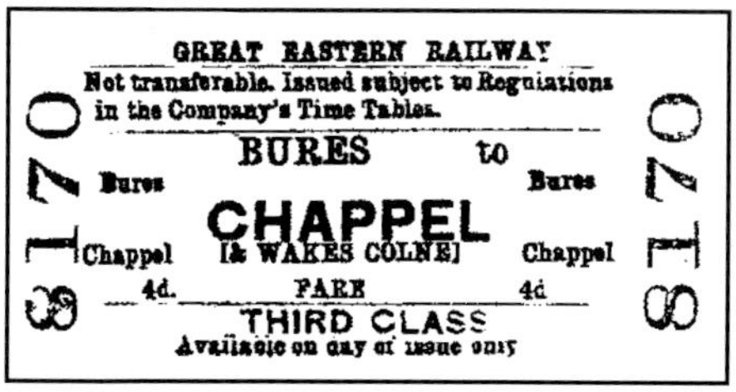

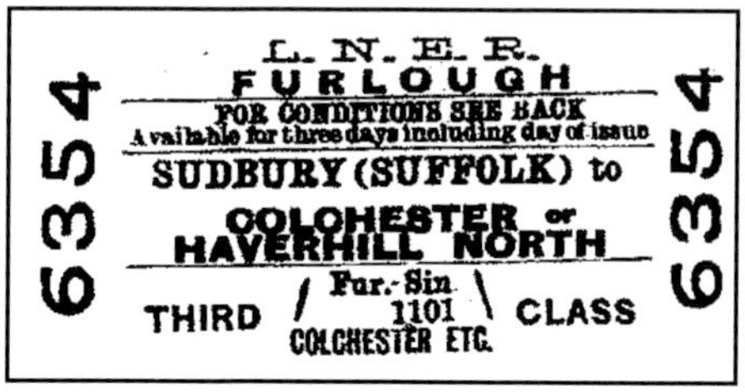

15. Running in from the south on 16th August 1957 is class J15 0-6-0 65465. The wartime oil tanks were built to the right of the train and at a lower level. They were fed by gravity from the siding. (B.Pask)

16. A northward view from the footbridge in June 1961 includes a DMU departing for the CV&H route, its point of divergence being just beyond the bridge. The goods yard contains much stock; it closed on 13th July 1964. The signal box had 44 levers. (D.C.Pearce)

17. This photograph from 9th September 1961 is unusual in that it includes a railbus in the goods yard. Both running lines were still in use as a DMU waits to leave for Marks Tey. On the right is the goods shed, which contained a 30cwt crane. The railbus is probably on layover between Colne Valley trips. (Colour-Rail.com)

18. A Craven DMU departs for Sudbury on 28th May 1973. The signal box had closed on 20th August 1967 and the loop was lifted subsequently. The Stour Valley Railway Preservation Society was formed in 1968 to conserve this area - hence the occupation of the box. The group was renamed the East Anglian Railway Museum in 1986 and growth on the site continued. It was leased from BR from December 1969. (Dr I.C.Scotchman)

19. The station had become unstaffed on 14th August 1966 and was photographed on 21st February 1976. On the left is the original building, which had become the house for the station master after the new one was completed. The footbridge has gone. (R.M.Casserley)

20. A southward panorama from the footbridge on 14th August 1987 shows some of the extensive trackwork of the museum.This includes the relaid loop under the coaches on the right. The replacement footbridge came from Sudbury in 1982. (R.M.Lyne)

21. Completion of a link with BR in 1985 was a major milestone in the museum's development and it is seen on 25th June 1988, as a DMU in NSE colours passes. The signal box from Mistley was added to the collection in 1985. (P.Hurst/Colour-Rail.com)

22. No. 150235 works the 15.44 from Marks Tey to Sudbury on 17th August 2001, while we marvel that the tightly packed museum can operate a passenger service within its confines. Sadly intransigent bureaucrats still prevent obviously remunerative heritage trains from being operated on the branch, although they were demonstrated on 21st and 29th December 1991 with 0-6-2T class N7 no. 69621. The platform on the left takes five coaches. (P.G.Barnes)

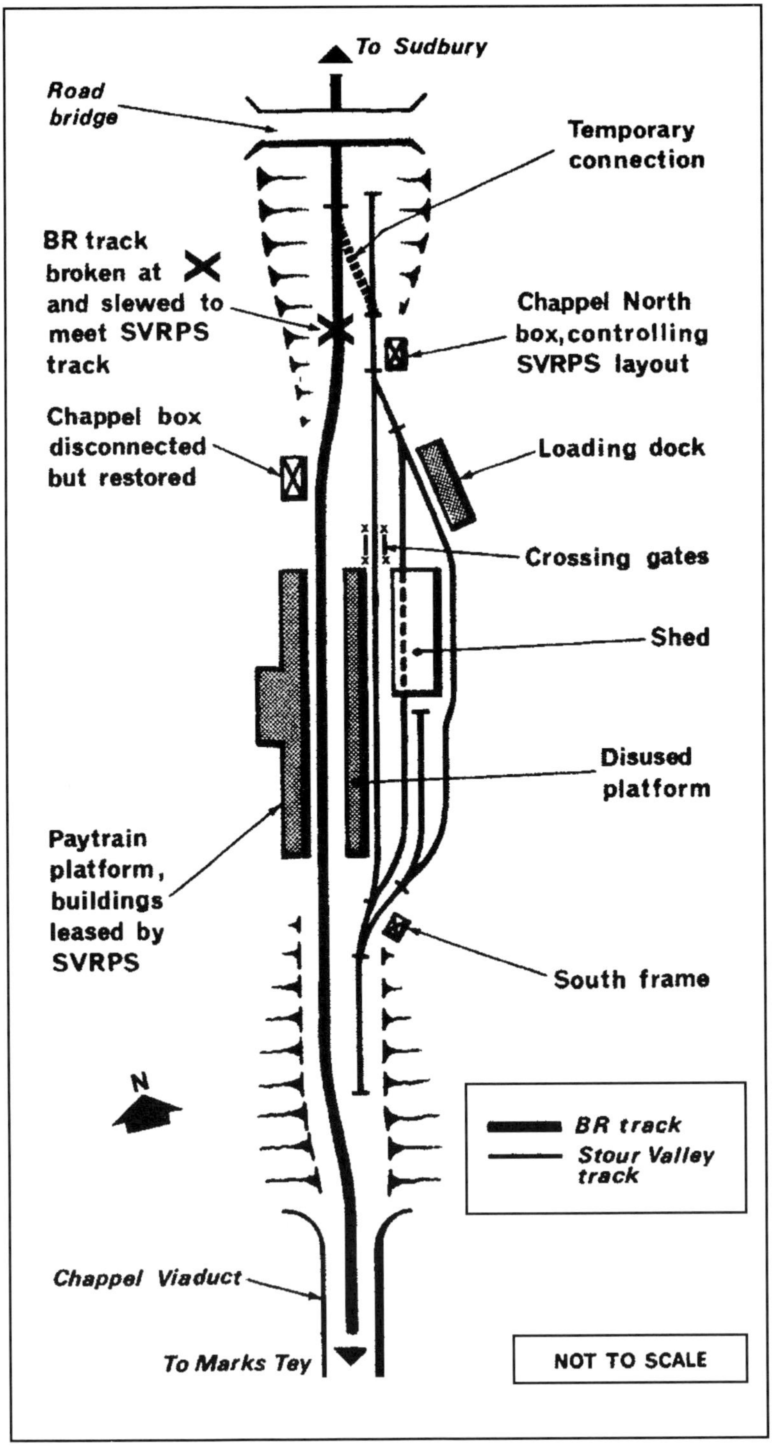

IV. The layout of the SVRPS is shown on 6th July 1975. The temporary slewing was undertaken to allow class S15 4-6-0 no. 30841 *Greene King* to travel to Shildon under its own steam. Inwards on the same day was a "Brighton Belle" car and two coaches. (Railway Magazine)

Telephone for opening hours
01206 242524
or visit -
www.earm.co.uk

BURES

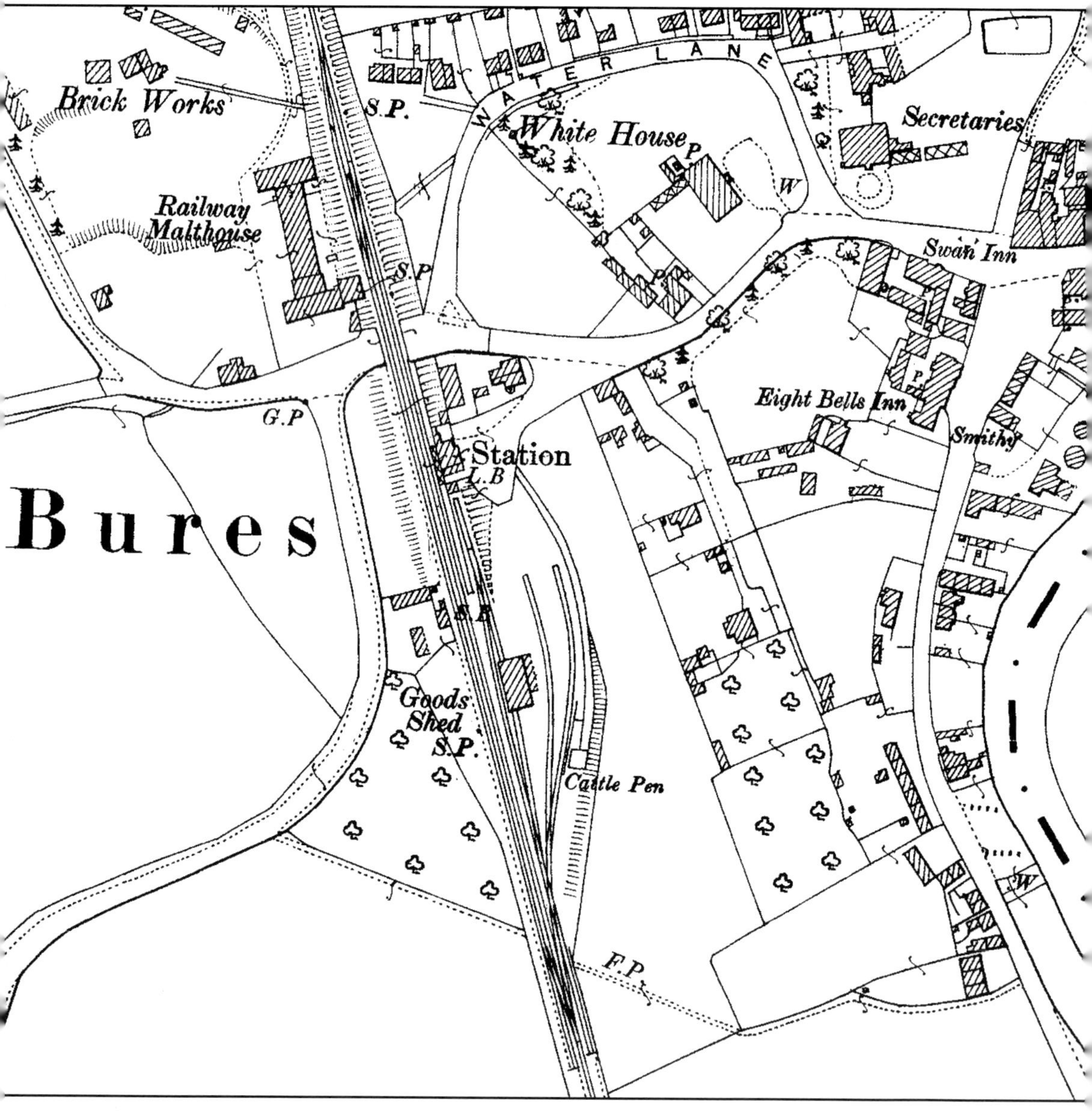

V. The 1904 survey has the county boundary dots and dashes in the River Stour. Residents numbered 511 in 1901 and 662 in 1961.

23. On the left is the station built by the CSVS&HR, while in the centre are semis for the staff. About four miles north of the station was Cornard Siding, which was usable until August 1967. (P.Laming coll.)

24. A little to the south of the station was Mount Bures level crossing, which had a resident crossing keeper and a 3-lever ground frame. An ex-GER class E4 2-4-0 is passing, sometime in 1948. (B.D.J.Walsh/Dr I.C.Scotchman)

25. The west side includes two of the white globes favoured by the LNER, plus an arch which probably once supported a bell. In the foreground is the loop, which was not signalled for use by passenger trains. (Dr I.C.Scotchman coll.)

26. Class J15 0-6-0 no. 65457 runs in during 1954 and we have the opportunity to see inside the goods shed with its 30cwt crane. Another example of a tender cab is visible. (B.D.J.Walsh/Dr I.C.Scotchman)

27. The signal box had been in the left foreground of this view from 28th October 1966. Its 26-lever frame from 1892 functioned until 6th September 1965. The goods yard had closed on 28th December 1964. The wooden part of the platform reduced the weight on the embankment. (B.W.L.Brooksbank)

28. No. 153311 runs in on 17th August 1994, working the 15.18 Marks Tey to Sudbury. An NSE seat is on the platform, which was then designated for four coaches. Class 153s had to be supplemented by buses from September 2000, as traffic had grown so much. (A.C.Hartless)

2. Haverhill to Glemsford

HAVERHILL NORTH

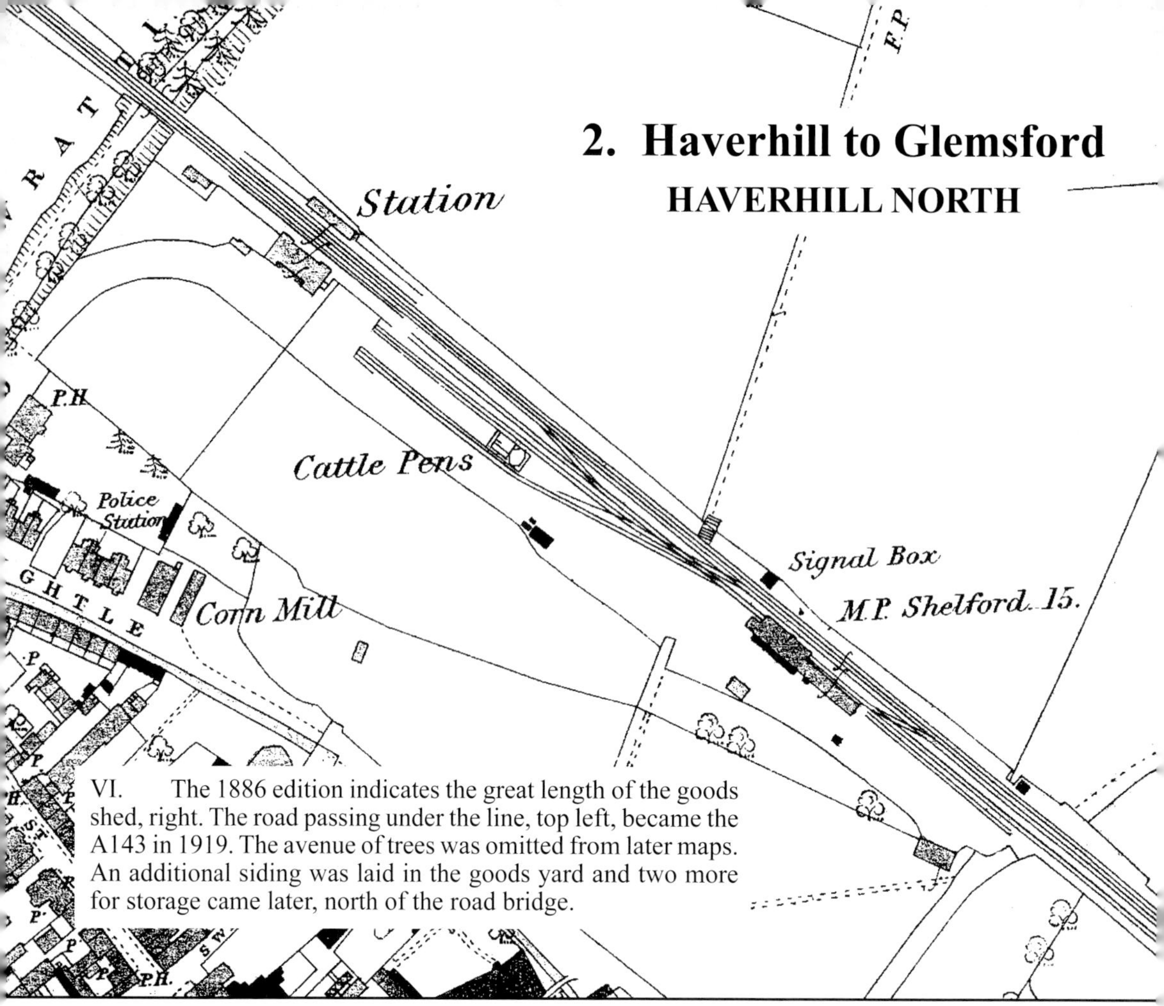

VI. The 1886 edition indicates the great length of the goods shed, right. The road passing under the line, top left, became the A143 in 1919. The avenue of trees was omitted from later maps. An additional siding was laid in the goods yard and two more for storage came later, north of the road bridge.

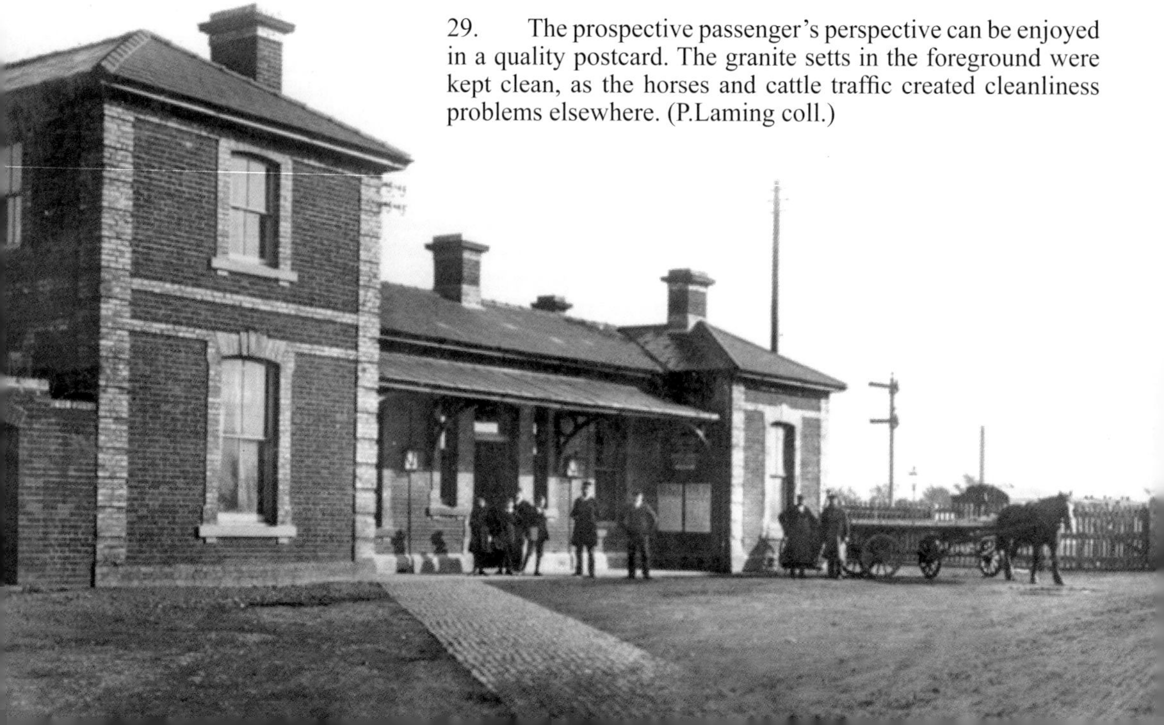

29. The prospective passenger's perspective can be enjoyed in a quality postcard. The granite setts in the foreground were kept clean, as the horses and cattle traffic created cleanliness problems elsewhere. (P.Laming coll.)

30. The staff and others pose on the other side of the building for another postcard. The horsebox has probably been detached from a recently departed train and will soon be pushed or horse hauled to the cattle dock. There was no horse landing here. Station Box is in the background. (P.Laming coll.)

31. We witness the connecting of trains on 19th October 1935. On the right is the 1.5pm Cambridge to Colchester train, via Sudbury, hauled by class E4 2-4-0 no. 7466. On the left is the 2.3pm departure to Chappel & Wakes Colne. (H.C.Casserley)

32. Decline had set in, the footbridge had lost its roof and the ballast was filthy. NORTH had been added to the name on 1st July 1923. The town housed 4862 in 1901 and 6620 in 1961. (Dr I.C.Scotchman coll.)

33. The steps nearest lead up to the goods office, the floor of which was on the same level as the 30cwt crane. On the right is the weigh house office. The suffix NORTH was dropped in May 1952. (Dr J.Westhall/A.Vaughan coll.)

HAVERHILL

34. We move nearer to the signal box, which replaced the small square one shown on the map in 1891. It had a 42-lever frame and was in use until 6th March 1967. Meat was notable in goods outward; for example, it amounted to 4400 tons in 1938. (Dr J.Westhall/A.Vaughan coll.)

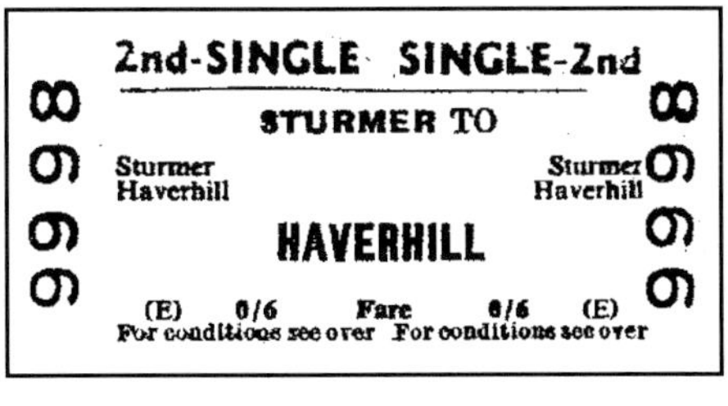

35. Included in this view northwestwards is the iron work of the bridge over the road and the crossover used by locomotives of trains terminating here, mostly from the Colne Valley. Next to the water column is the fire-devil, which was lit to prevent it freezing.
(Dr J.Westhall/A.Vaughan coll.)

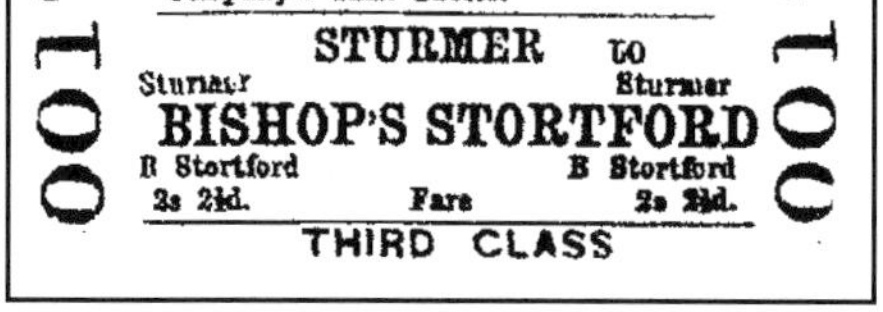

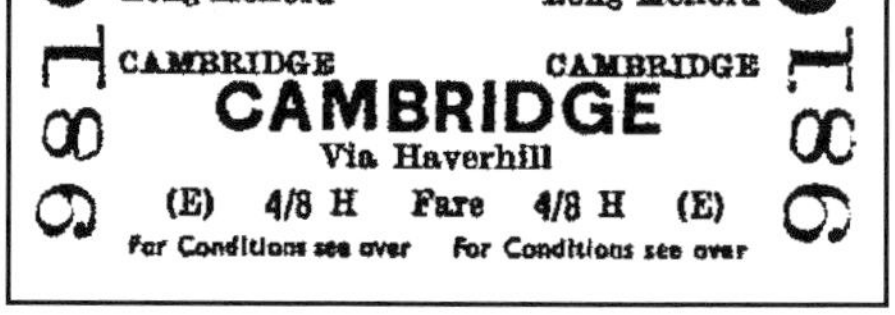

36. Class J15 0-6-0 no. 65390 blows off, ready to leave at 5.10pm with the Cambridge to Colchester via Sudbury service on 23rd May 1956. The cattle pens are included in the view, as is an early container. (H.Bowtell/S.Garrett.coll.)

37. Class E4 2-4-0 no. 62789 waits by the water column on 27th May 1957, heading the 1.33pm Cambridge to Colchester. The end loading dock is on the left. (R.M.Casserley)

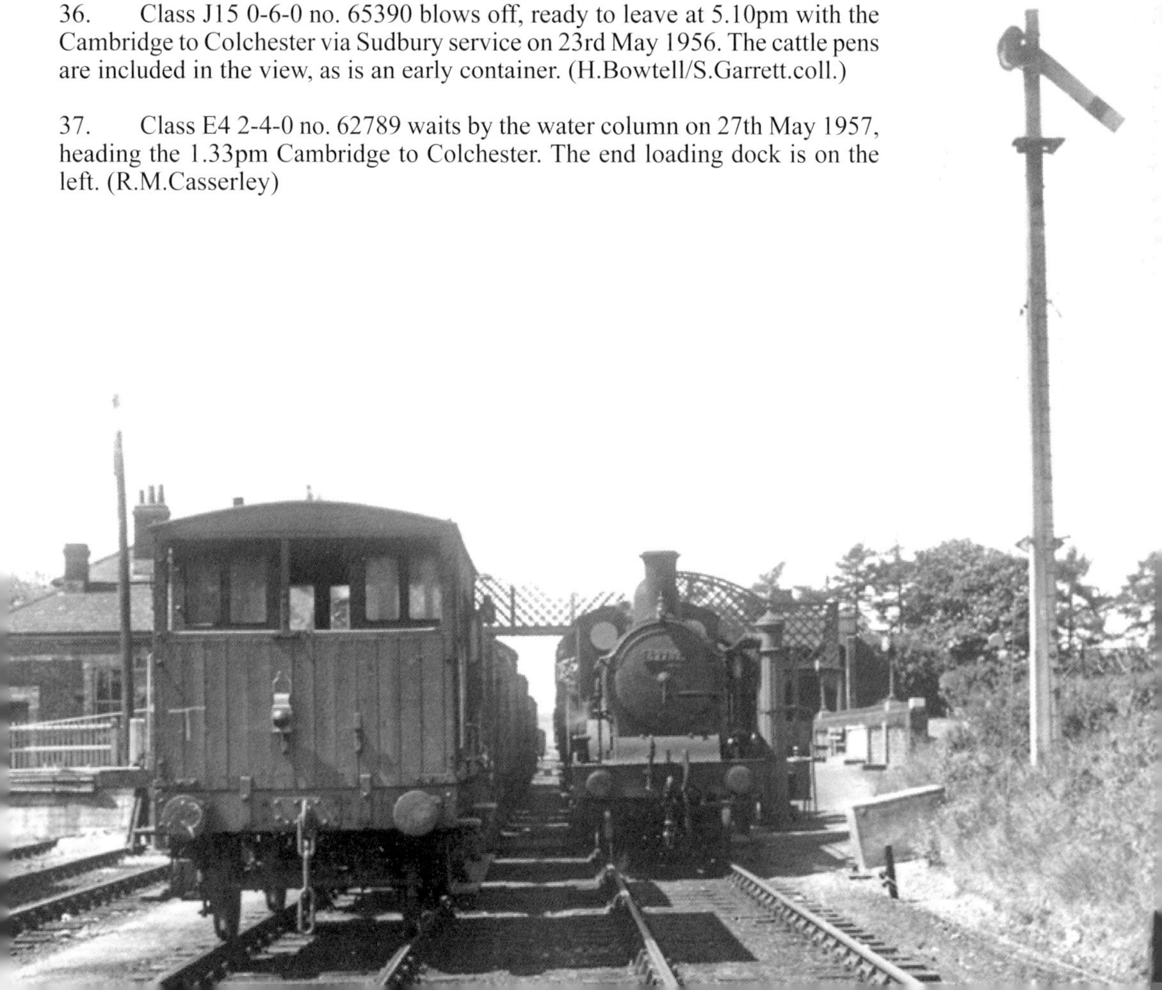

38. The RCTS "Northern & Eastern" railtour was hauled by class J15 0-6-0 no. 65440 on 10th August 1958. The water tank does not appear clearly in the other views. The footbridge dates from about 1893. (B.W.L.Brooksbank)

39. A well balanced photograph from the 1960s has good lighting, sufficient to show the bookstall in detail. The railbus was made in Germany by Waggon Maschinenbau.
(Lens of Sutton coll.)

40. We finish with two pictures from 23rd December 1961. The footbridge reflects in a window of a DMU running on the long loop. The station was unstaffed from 14th August 1966 and closed on 6th March 1967. The site is now occupied by a branch of Tesco and there is no evidence of the railway. (B.Pask)

41. Class B1 4-6-0 no. 61005 is in the same position as the leading coach of the DMU in the previous picture. In those days, freight trains such as this had no continuous brakes and were loose coupled. The goods yard also closed on 6th March 1967. (B.Pask)

HAVERHILL CVR

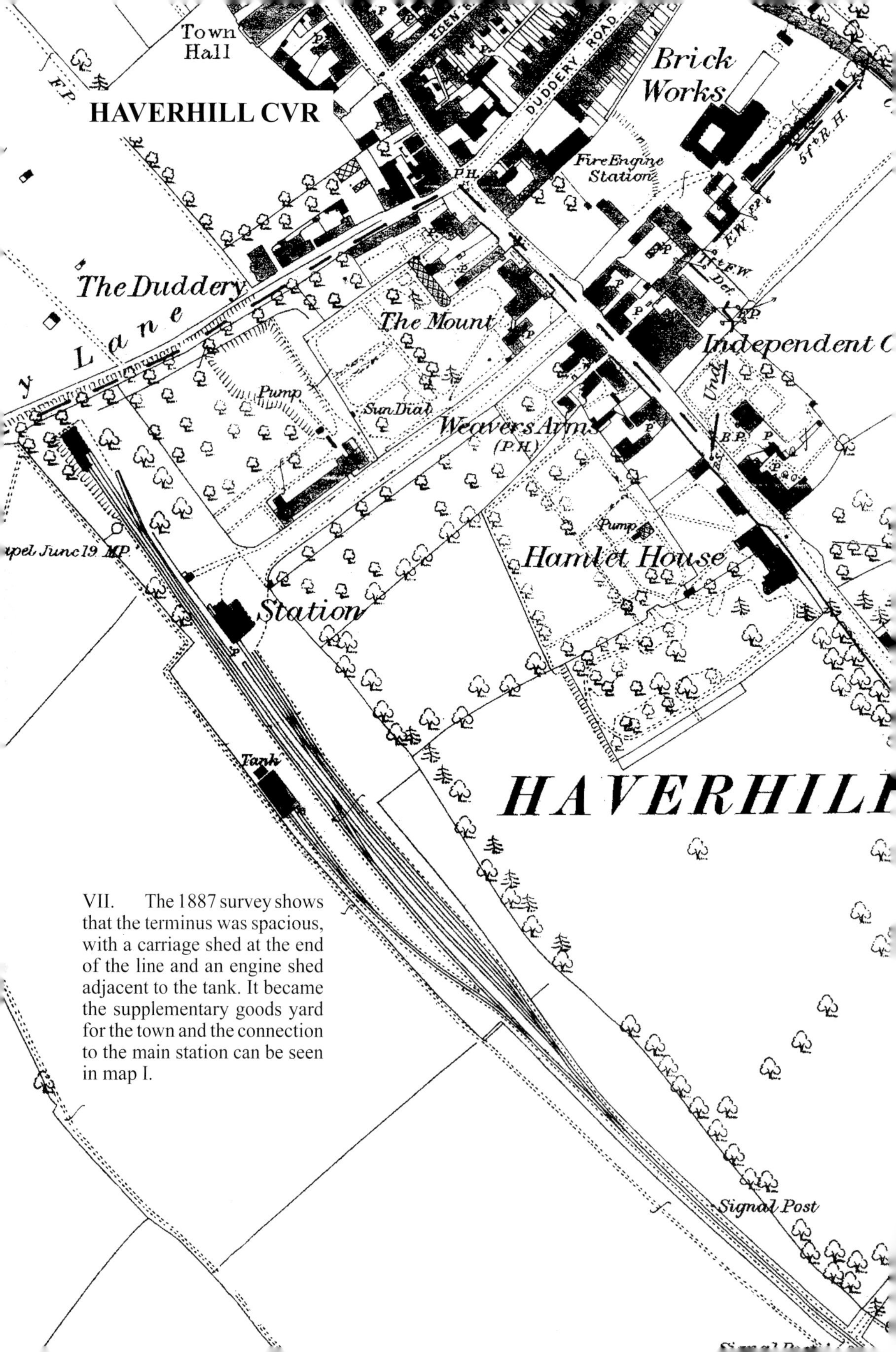

VII. The 1887 survey shows that the terminus was spacious, with a carriage shed at the end of the line and an engine shed adjacent to the tank. It became the supplementary goods yard for the town and the connection to the main station can be seen in map I.

42. The goods shed is seen in about 1912, with the passenger station beyond. The latter closed on 14th July 1924, but most trains prior to that had run to the other station to provide connections. (Lens of Sutton coll.)

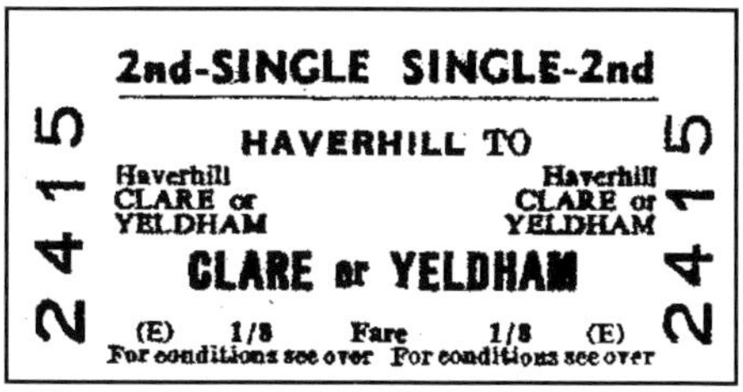

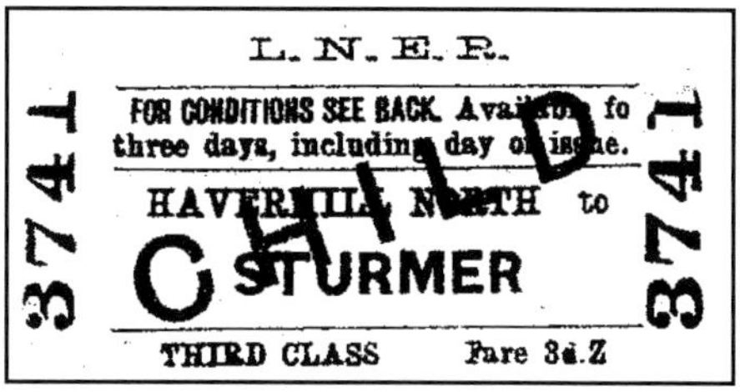

43. This was the neglected scene on 27th May 1957, viewed in the opposite direction, with the water tank surprisingly still standing. There was a 15cwt crane in the goods shed. There is now no trace of either station. (R.M.Casserley)

44. The area was known as SOUTH for goods purposes from 1st February 1925. The yard was photographed on 23rd December 1961 and was closed on 19th April 1965. The connection to NORTH was officially abolished in August 1965. (B.Pask)

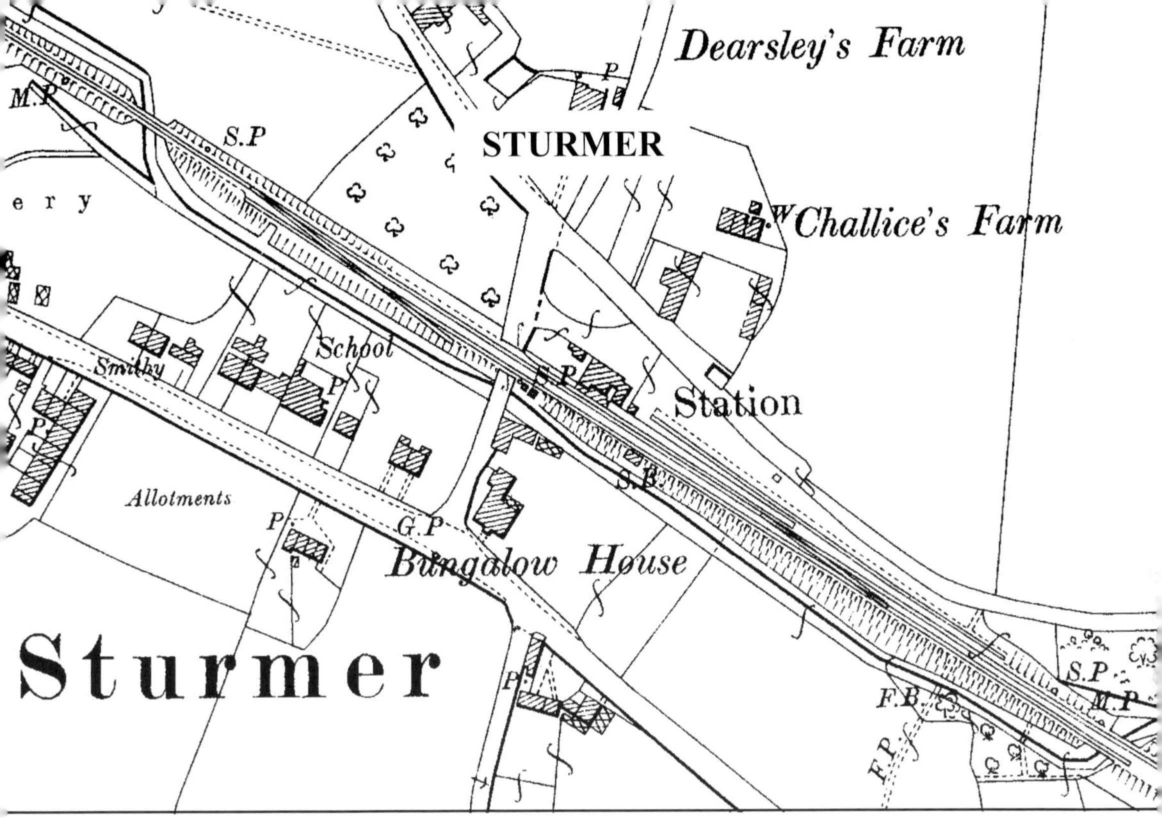

VIII. The 1904 map includes a signal box. It was in use from before 1892 until 1931 and had 20 levers. The population was steady: 328 in 1901 and 321 in 1961.

45. The photograph is from the 1966-67 period. Staffing ceased on 28th January 1963 and the goods yard closed on 25th June 1962. The building still stands, in use as a dwelling. (Lens of Sutton coll.)

46. The discs were commonly known as targets. Here there was an unusually high one. It seems that there was a hump in the track. The wagon is in the goods loop, not a siding.
(Norfolk Railway Society)

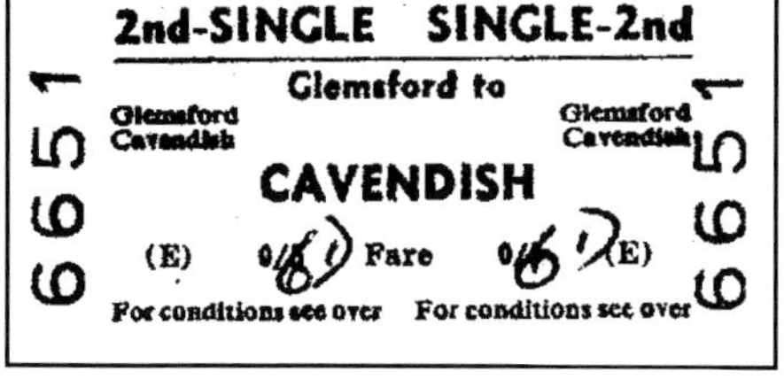

STOKE (SUFFOLK)

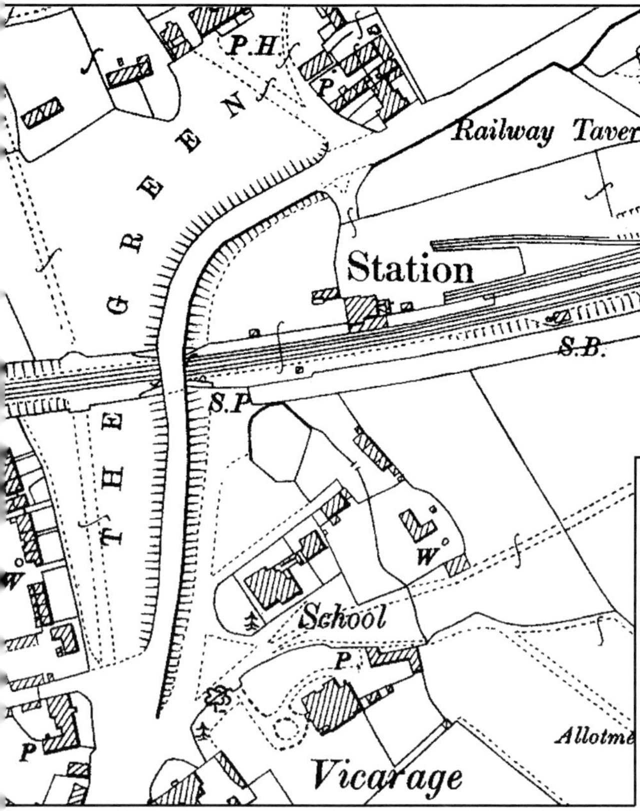

IX. The 1904 survey shows the four essentials of a village. Only the smithy and the post office are off this extract. There were 602 folk in 1901, but only 393 in 1961.

47. The approach to the bridge made a good vantage point for this Summer panorama, when all sash windows were open to their maximum. One presumes that the milk churns were empty. Evident is the busy goods yard. (P.Laming coll.)

48. In this view from the bridge is the 20-lever signal box, which served from prior to 1892 until 18th October 1931. It is opposite the goods yard; the line in front of it is a goods loop. (P.Laming coll.)

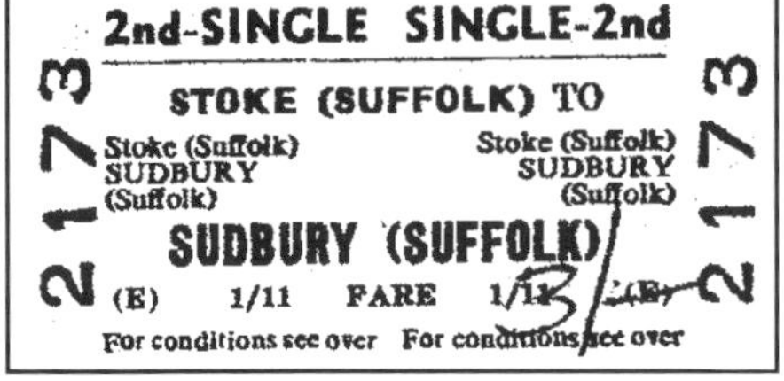

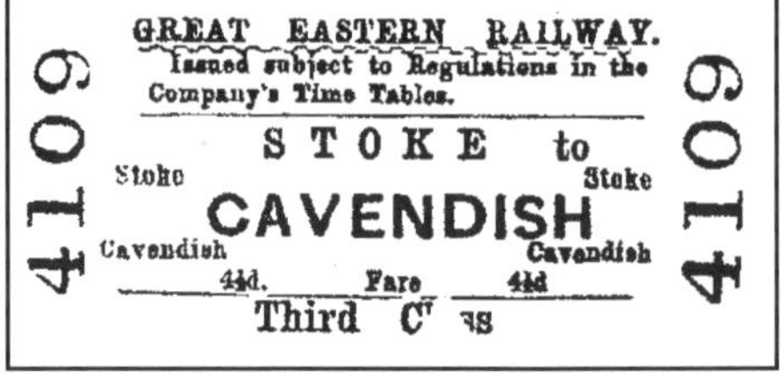

49. This must be a pre-1931 postcard, as a signal is still present. Station staffing ended on 28th January 1963. The station was known as Stoke-by-Clare in its early years, although not officially. (P.Laming coll.)

50. The suffix (SUFFOLK) was applied from June 1932 until closure. This view is from the final years and grain traffic seems to still be heavy. The goods yard closed on 19th April 1965. (Lens of Sutton coll.)

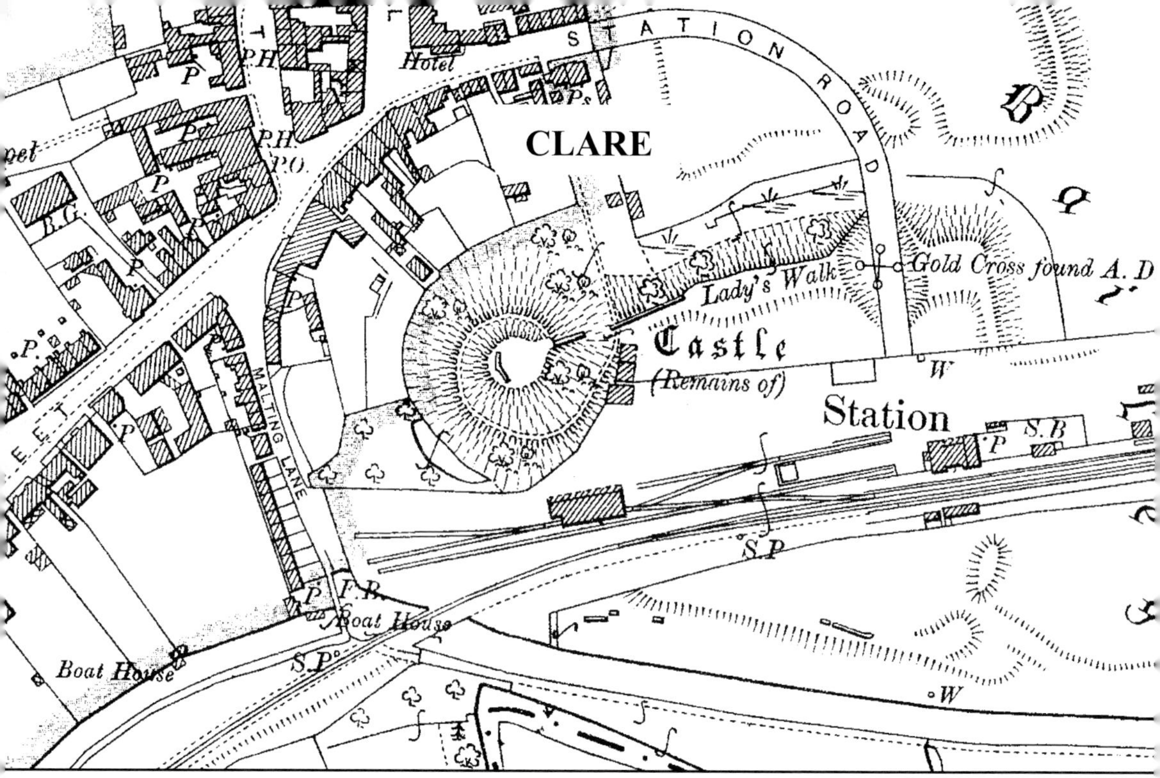

X. The 1904 edition reveals two boat houses and that both the station and station road were built on the castle bailey. This is the biggest community between Haverhill and Sudbury. The folk numbered 1582 in 1901 and 1328 in 1961.

51. The locomotive is close to the goods shed as it approaches the short platform. The bridge in the foreground is over a short tributary of the River Stour. Goods traffic ceased on 12th September 1966. (P.Laming coll.)

52. This closer view of the goods shed shows a fresh doorway and class J20 0-6-0 no. 64696 shunting on 30th May 1960. There was a resident crane rated at 30cwt, but a portable one stands near the castle mound for a heavier item. (Colour-Rail.com.)

53. Twelve months later, the fine quoins were photographed from the barrow crossing, which was also used by passengers. The staff crossing is opposite the signal box, which had 25 levers and was in use until the end. (P.J.Kelley)

54. The structures on both platforms were recorded on 5th May 1967 and both were conserved subsequently. The goods shed later contained a display of local railway historical material. (B.Pask)

55. The exterior is seen on the same day. In 1972, the building became a house for the warden of the Clare Castle Country Park and is thus likely to remain intact. (B.Pask)

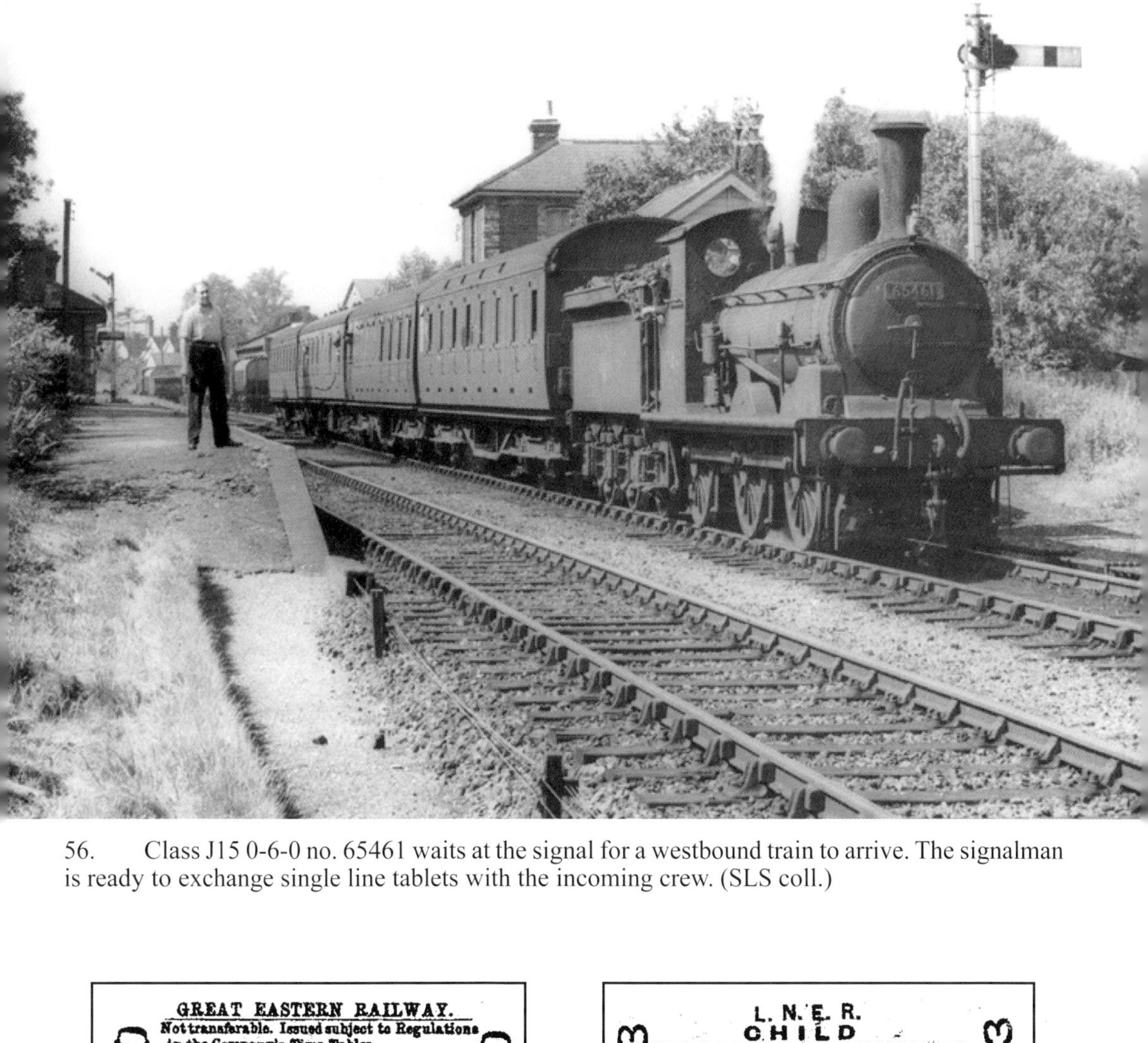

56. Class J15 0-6-0 no. 65461 waits at the signal for a westbound train to arrive. The signalman is ready to exchange single line tablets with the incoming crew. (SLS coll.)

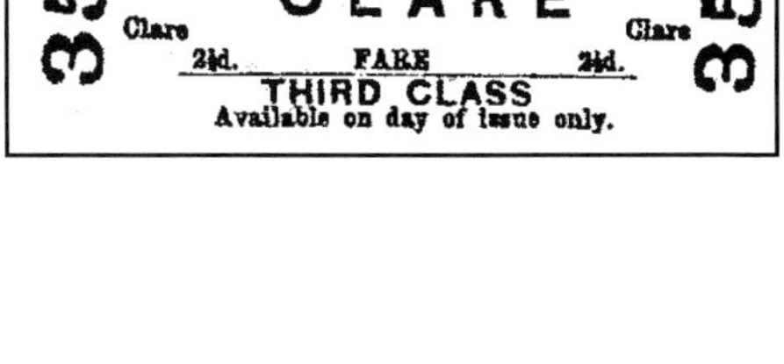

CAVENDISH

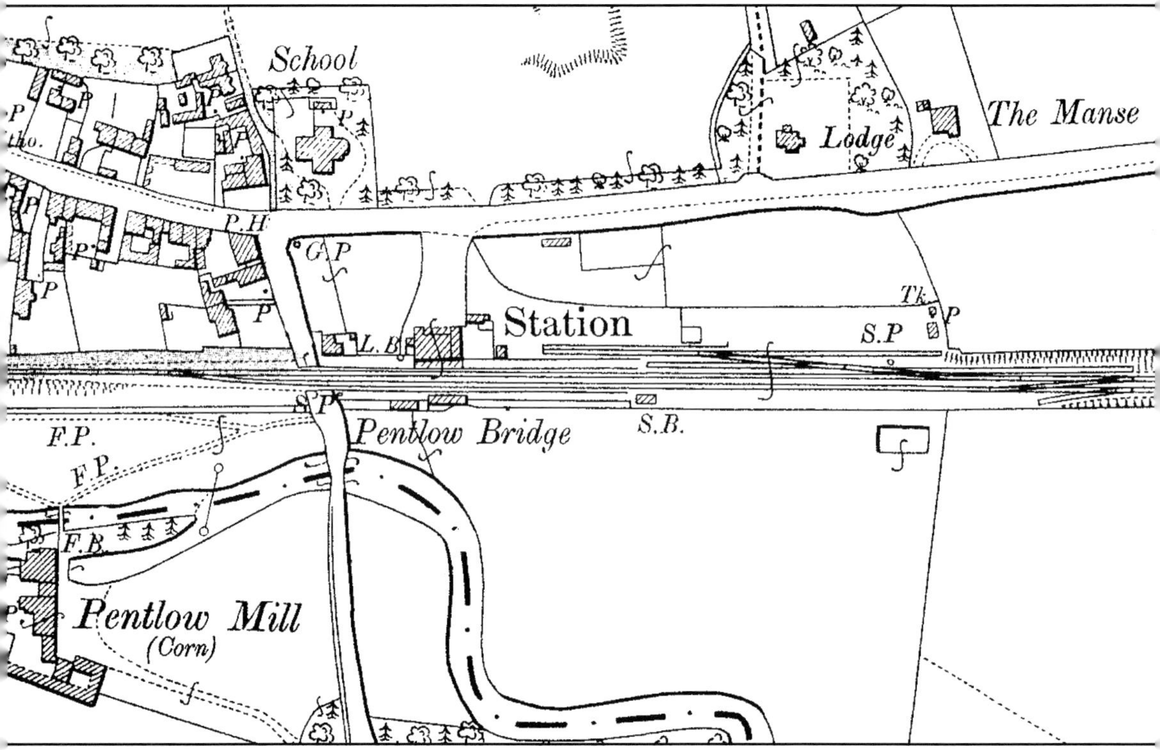

XI. The county boundary is still close to the line as we travel east. The Manse is the term used for the residence provided for the Non-conformist minister. He would have cared for 897 souls in 1901 and 701 in 1961; the map is from 1904.

57. This panorama is from the vicinity of the mill and includes one of the massive wooden posts provided for the level crossing gates. (P.Laming coll.)

58. The two posts are clearer in this record of no. 425, a GER 2-4-0 of class E4. The station master was honoured with a fine dwelling and it still stands. (P.Laming coll.)

59. A view east includes the signal box, which was in use by 1892. Its 22-lever frame was functional until line closure in 1967. Housing now covers the site. (B.Pask)

60. An early 1960s record fails to show any provision for ladies. These were often discreetly signed within the booking hall. The provision of a letter box on the platform was less common than on the station approach. (Lens of Sutton coll.)

→ 61. The north elevation is seen on 5th June 1965, together with the goods yard gates. These were normally locked outside working hours, but freight traffic had ceased on 28th December 1964. (R.M.Casserley)

→ 62. The station became unstaffed on 4th August 1966 and so the gents had lost its sign. Splendid views from the front seats of DMUs were some compensation for other losses in that era. (W.A.Camwell/SLS coll.)

GLEMSFORD

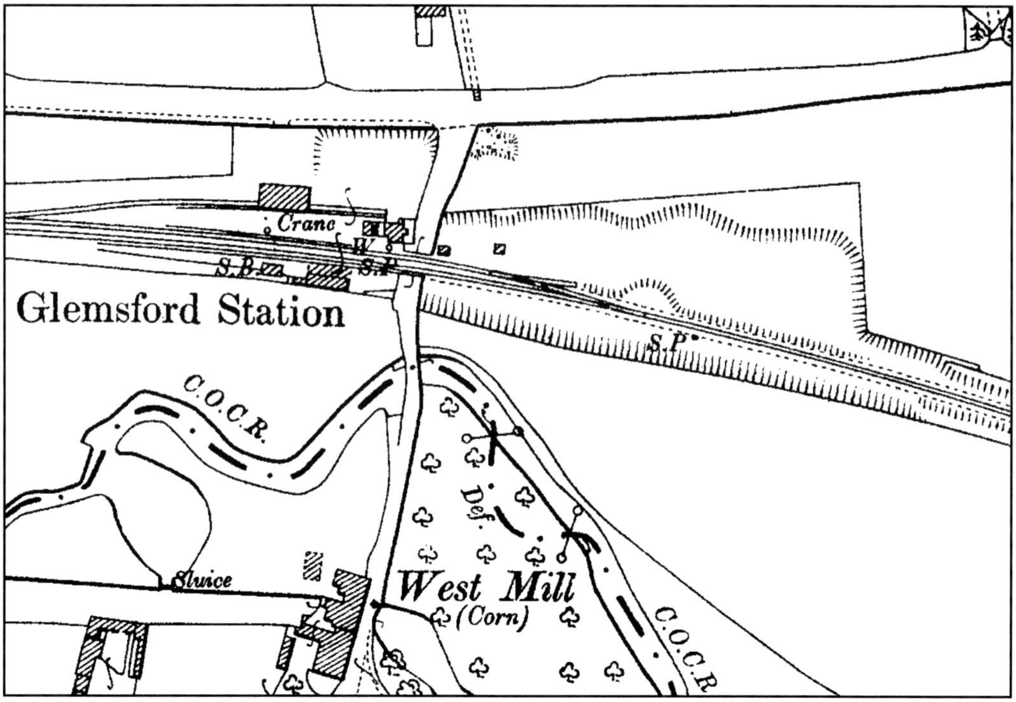

XII. Another 1904 map and this also includes a mill near the station. The latter opened later than the others, in about July 1866. It served 1975 folk in 1901 and 1365 in 1961. The village was one mile to the north.

63. A view south from the road junction at the top of the map has the level crossing and the spacious house for the station master on the left. The goods shed is on the right. (P.Laming coll.)

64. Only the line on the left was used for passenger trains, the other being a goods loop, confirmed by a loading gauge. The building on the right appears to be for the gatekeeper. (P.Laming coll.)

65. The dock has two faces and the 30cwt crane is near the right one. The end is nigh, as weeds take over the yard. (Dr I.C.Scotchman coll.)

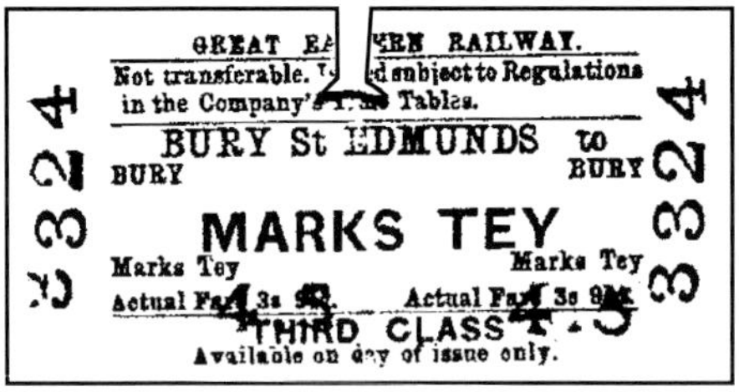

66. Goods traffic continued until 12th September 1966, this view being from about 1962. The signal position is remote from the line to which it applied. The box had 22 levers and remained in use until 6th March 1967. (Lens of Sutton coll.)

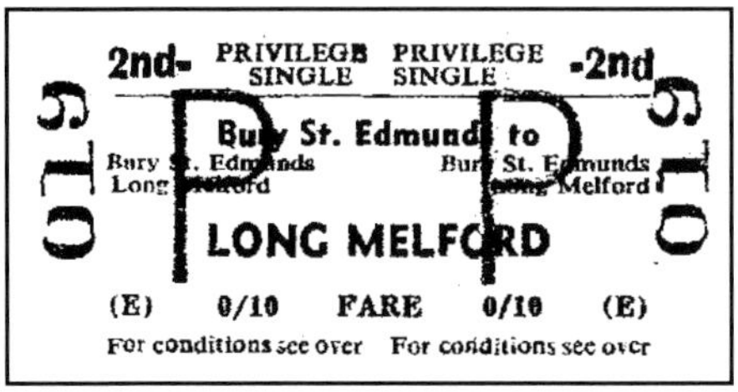

➔ 67. There was no staff after 15th August 1966, but all seemed to be in good order when photographed on 5th May 1967. This building was demolished, but the house was not. (B.Pask)

CLEMSFORD

3. Bury St. Edmunds to Long Melford

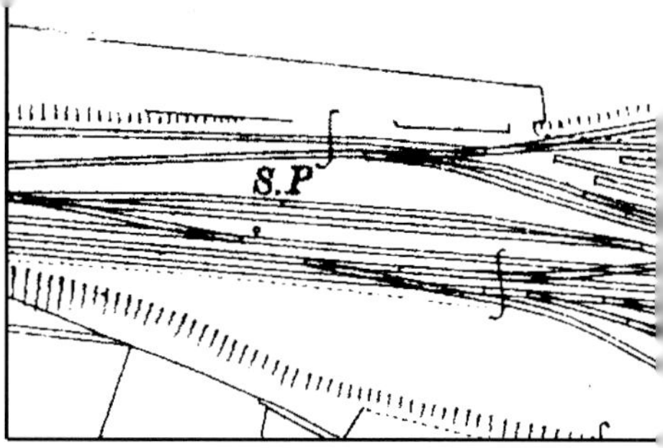

BURY ST. EDMUNDS

BURY ST. EDMUNDS.

POPULATION.—13,318.

Distance from station, ½ mile.

A telegraph station.

HOTELS.—Angel; Bell.

MARKET DAYS.—Wednesday and Saturday.

FAIRS.—October 2nd and December 1st.

MONEY ORDER OFFICE.

BANKERS.—Oakes, Bevan, and Co.; John Worlledge and Co.; National Provincial Bank of England; Harvey and Hudsons.

An old Saxon town and parliamentary borough, situated in so healthy a spot that it has been called the Montpelier of England, in a beautiful part of West Suffolk, founded by Canute along with an abbey, to commemorate the martyrdom of Edmund, a King of East Anglia, by the Danes, in the year 870. This became one of the largest and most richly endowed monasteries in the kingdom, being "505 feet long and 212 wide, with twelve chapels and churches, cloisters, offices, &c., attached, forming a little town in itself. The abbot was mitred, and reigned over an establishment of monks, chaplains, and servants, amounting to 200. He had a mint and a *gallows* in the town, of which he was chief magistrate, with a jurisdiction over the entire liberty (*i.e.*, six hundreds and a half in this shire), the royalties of which together with 53 knights' fees, and other possessions, made a revenue equivalent to £50,000 in the present day" *(Sharp's British Gazetteer)*. Of this luxurious house, which our early sovereigns frequently visited, all that now remains are part of a tower, a beautiful Norman gate, 80 feet high, the abbey church, and gate.

Bury stands on the slope of a gentle and well cultivated sand-hill, the best prospect of it being from the Vinefield. *St. Mary's* old parish church contains the effigies of Henry VIII.'s sister, Mary, who married Charles Brandon, Duke of Suffolk, and of Reeve, the last Abbot of Bury. At one time it possessed 40 churches and religious foundations. The *Shire Hall* occupies the place of St. Margaret's church. The *Guildhall* has an ancient porch. There is a large *County Prison*, and a *Bridewell* in the Norman style; a handsome *County Hospital*. The *Grammar School* has produced many eminent men, such as Archbishop Sancroft, Dr. Blomfield (late Bishop of London), a native, Lord Keeper North, Sir Samuel Romilly, Cumberland, the dramatist, &c. Bloomfield the poet was born at Honington. The famous Bishop Gardiner of Mary's time, was also a native.

Extract from Bradshaw's Guide for 1866. (Reprinted by Middleton Press 2011)

68. The south elevation must be one of the finest of any country station in England. No doubt the postcard impressed many recipients. The end of a train is included. There was a temporary station until this one was completed in November 1847. (P.Laming coll.)

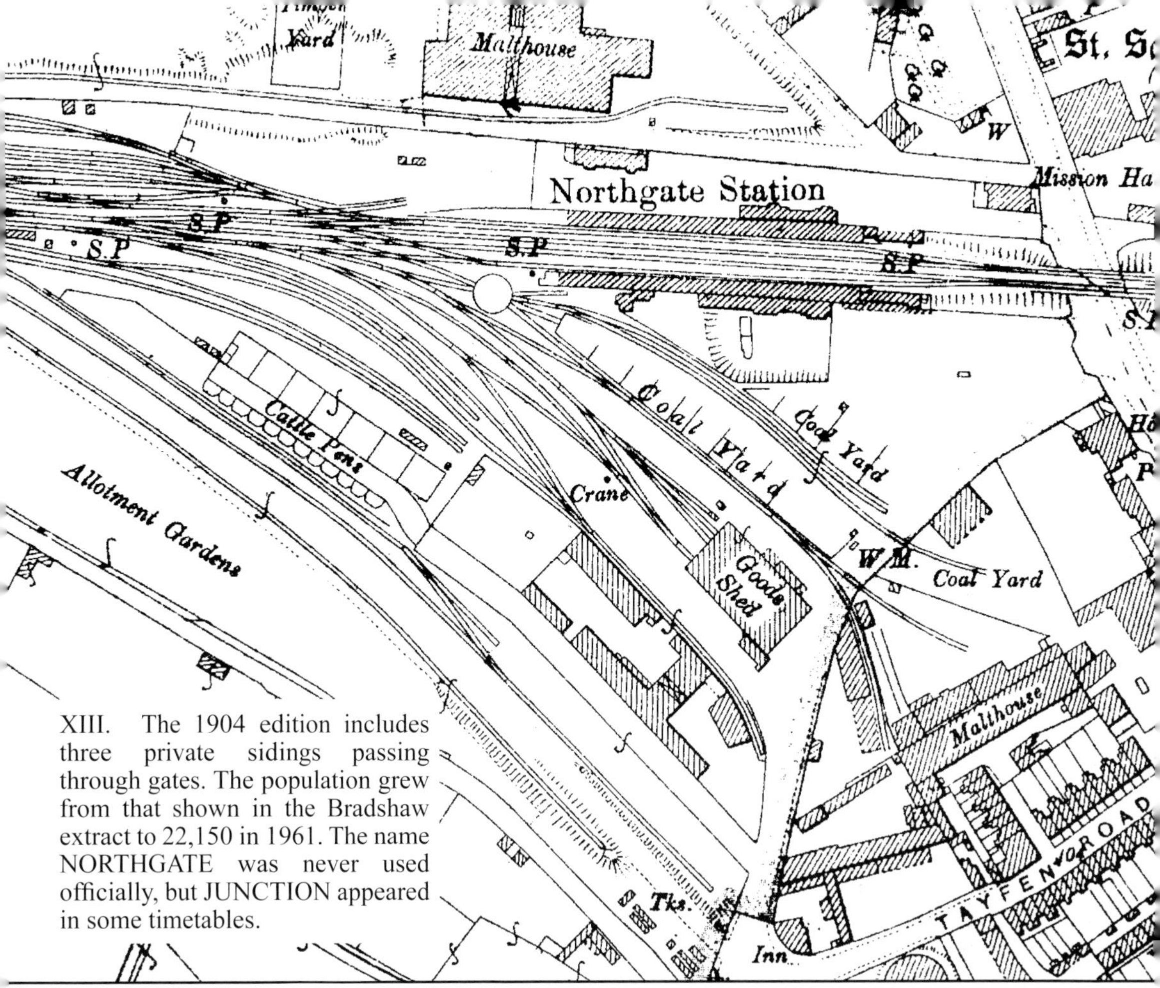

XIII. The 1904 edition includes three private sidings passing through gates. The population grew from that shown in the Bradshaw extract to 22,150 in 1961. The name NORTHGATE was never used officially, but JUNCTION appeared in some timetables.

69. This view is eastwards from the station towards the junction. The left signal arm is for Thetford, the centre one for Ipswich and the right one for the Sudbury trains. In the distance is Junction Box, which had 38 levers and worked until 8th May 1983.
(Dr J.Westhall/A.Vaughan coll.)

↑ 70. Arriving at the west end on 1st August 1933 is class B12 4-6-0 no. 8508. The inspection pit on the left was also used for lubrication purposes. The centre roads were provided for through freight trains; certainly forward thinking in those early days. (D.C.Pearce coll.)

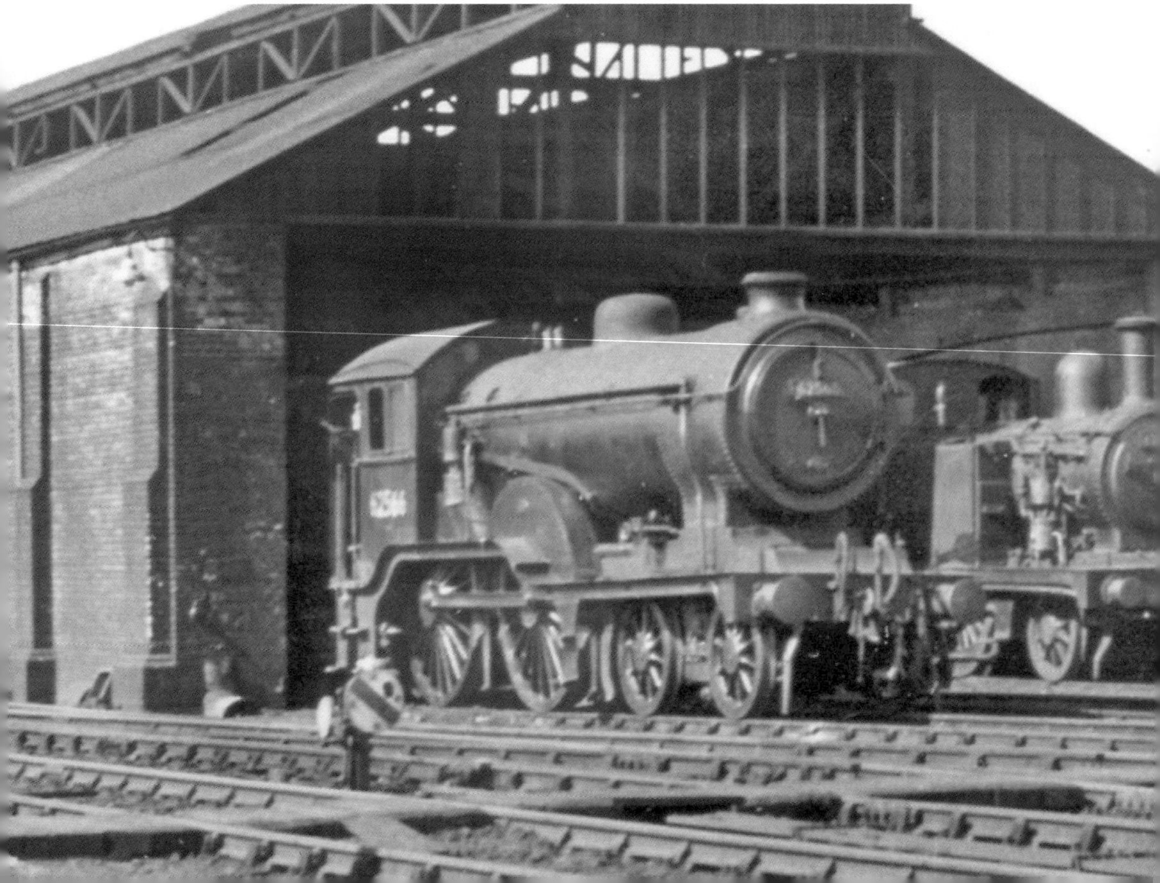

↓ 71. Present on 19th September 1953 are class D16/3 4-4-0 no. 62566 and class F6 2-4-2T nos 67236 and 67222. The shed was coded 31E from 1949 until 1959, when it closed. It had 14 locomotives in 1950. (H.C.Casserley)

72. The west end of the layout was in open country when photographed on 26th May 1957, with class N7/4 0-6-2T no. 69619 in attendance. The curved white handle is for pushing the turntable and the straight one is the brake. (H.K.Fairey/Colour-Rail.com)

73. The site was used for berthing diesels after the end of steam and one is seen in 1960, after much of the roof had been removed. (D.C.Pearce)

74. Few railways offered a choice of toilet window shapes, but the LNER was generous in this regard. A Brush Type 2 (later class 31) is ready to depart for Ipswich on 8th June 1961, while a Cravens DMU displays a rear lamp. (Colour-Rail.com)

75. By 1st August 1975, no trace was left of the through lines, but some freight was still seen. No. 08716 rests between duties at the down platform. This was limited to eight coaches and the up one to five by 2006. (D.C.Pearce)

76. The goods yard is seen on the same day, as is Yard Box. It was built in 1888 and was fitted with a 54-lever frame in 1943. Much extra wartime traffic was handled at that time, both here and at the nearby stations, mainly for RAF airfields. (D.C.Pearce)

77. No. 153326 was working the 14.15 Ipswich to Peterborough service when photographed on 27th June 1996. A massive restoration programme on the station had been completed in March 1995. Stone traffic began again in December 1997, Tarmac using one of the five sidings remaining south of the station. (A.C.Hartless)

BURY (EAST GATE)

XIV. History abounds in this extract from 1904. The long single siding is in a cutting and its purpose seems unrecorded.

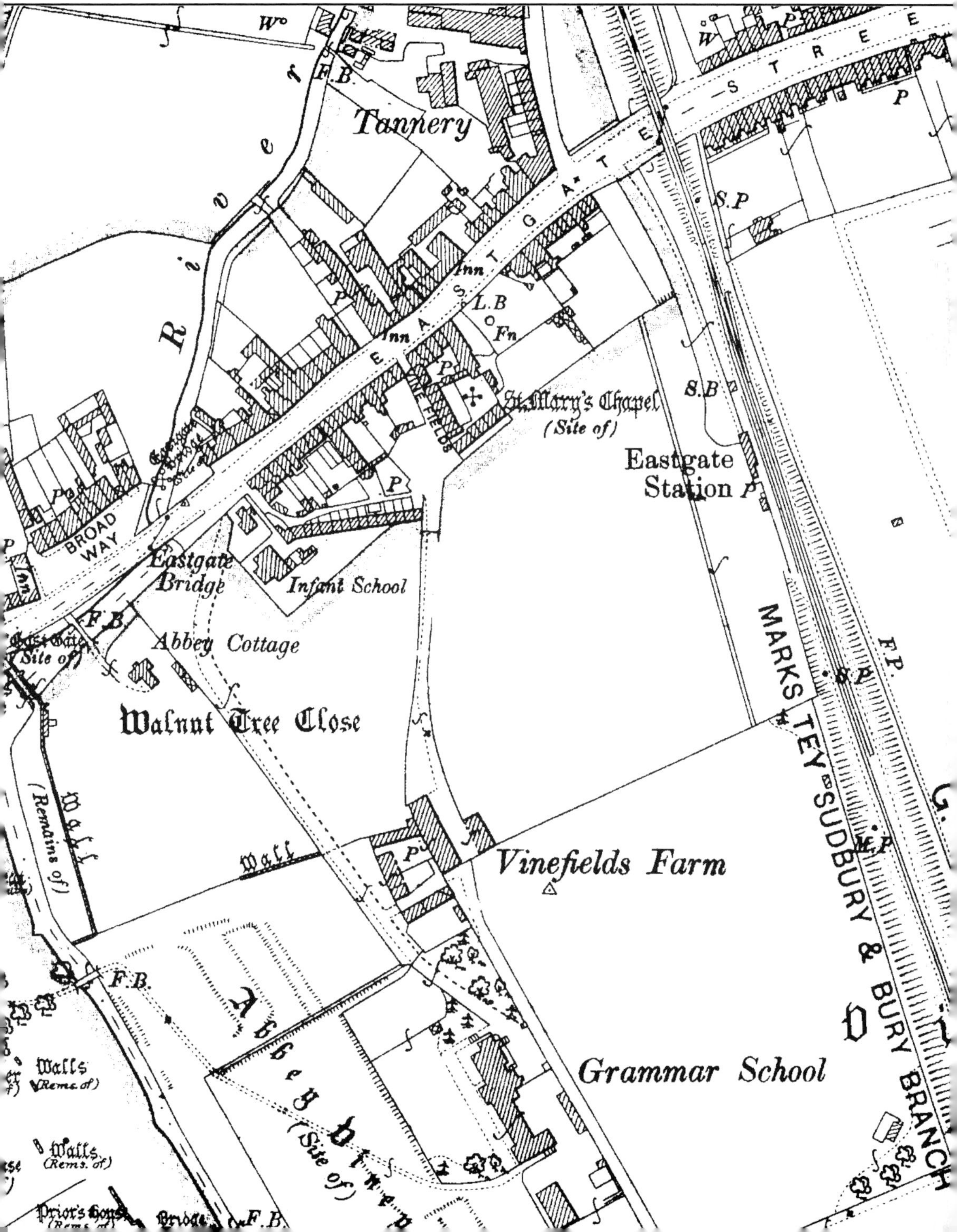

78. The station opened on 9th August 1865, but it was not a commercial success, closing on 1st May 1909. Whiskers prevail. (P.Laming coll.)

79. The entire route south hereof was engineered for double track, but only this part received it. A ground frame was in the hut between about 1885 and 1909. The bridge is just off the lower right corner of the map. The platform was used for an agricultural show in July 1914. (P.Laming coll.)

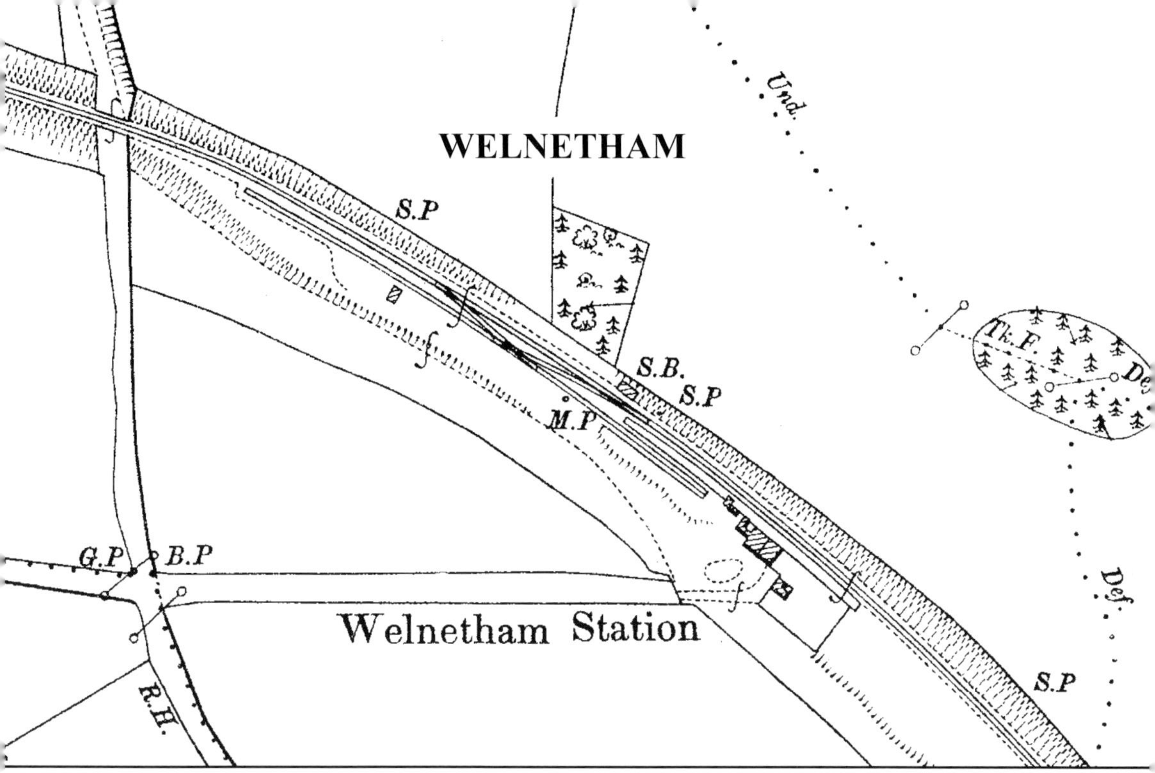

XV. The 1904 edition shows no habitation nearby. The tiny village had recorded 73 residents three years earlier.

80. Familiar architecture is seen again, with only the lampman's ladder justifying comment. The hut on the right was termed "Signal Box" by the cartographer. It contained 18 levers from 1892 until 1926 and three thereafter. (Norfolk Railway Society)

81. A view in the other direction is from the ground frame and includes the full range of chimney pots. The hut was probably used for parcel traffic, as it is unheated. (Norfolk Railway Society)

May 1960

LONG MELFORD and BURY ST. EDMUNDS

Miles		Week Days only						
		am H		pm F	pm	pm		
	3 London (L'pool St.) dep	4 35	..	12C38	1C30	4J58	..	..
		D		D	D			
—	**Long Melford** .... dep	7 54	....	2 31	3 45	6 56	....	....
5¼	Lavenham	8 6	..	2 40	3 54	7 5	..	..
8½	Cockfield (Suffolk)	8 12	....	2 46	4 0	7 12	....	....
11½	Welnetham	8 17	..	2 51	4 5	7 17	..	..
16½	**Bury St. Edmunds** .. arr	8 26	....	3 0	4 14	7 26	....	....

Miles		Week Days only						
		am D B		pm D		pm D K		pm G
—	**Bury St. Edmunds** .. dep	7 45	..	3 4	..	4 23	..	5 49
5	Welnetham	7 53	....	3 13	....	4 31	....	....
8	Cockfield (Suffolk)	7 59	..	3 19	..	4 37	..	6 2
11¼	Lavenham	8 5	....	3 24	....	4 43	....	6 8
16½	**Long Melford** .. .. arr	8 14	..	3 33	..	4 52	..	6 17
	3 London (L'pool St.) arr	10 0	....	5 40	....	7 40	....	9 10

D Diesel Train

B Through Train to Colchester arr 8 51 am (Table 22)

C Via Colchester

F Through Train from Colchester dep 1 52 pm (Table 22)

G Through Train to Sudbury arr 6 24 pm (Table 22)

H Through Train from Mark's Tey dep 7 27 am (Table 22)

J On Saturdays dep 4 36 pm via Colchester

K Through Train to Colchester arr 5 29 pm (Table 22)

82. Class J15 0-6-0 no. 65477 makes a courtesy call on 22nd May 1959 with the evening train from Long Melford to Bury St. Edmunds. It seems that only the photographer benefitted from the stop. (J.Langford)

83. The last call by any train was made on 4th June 1961. The special was hauled by no. D5537 amidst a fine floral display. (B.Pask)

84. No polite adjectives can be used for the growth recorded on 5th June 1965. Wagon load traffic had continued to the siding until 13th July 1964, but there had been no staff since 1961. (R.M.Casserley)

85. The exterior was photographed on the same day. The building became a house, but the yard was used for a rubbish pulveriser from 1984. (R.M.Casserley)

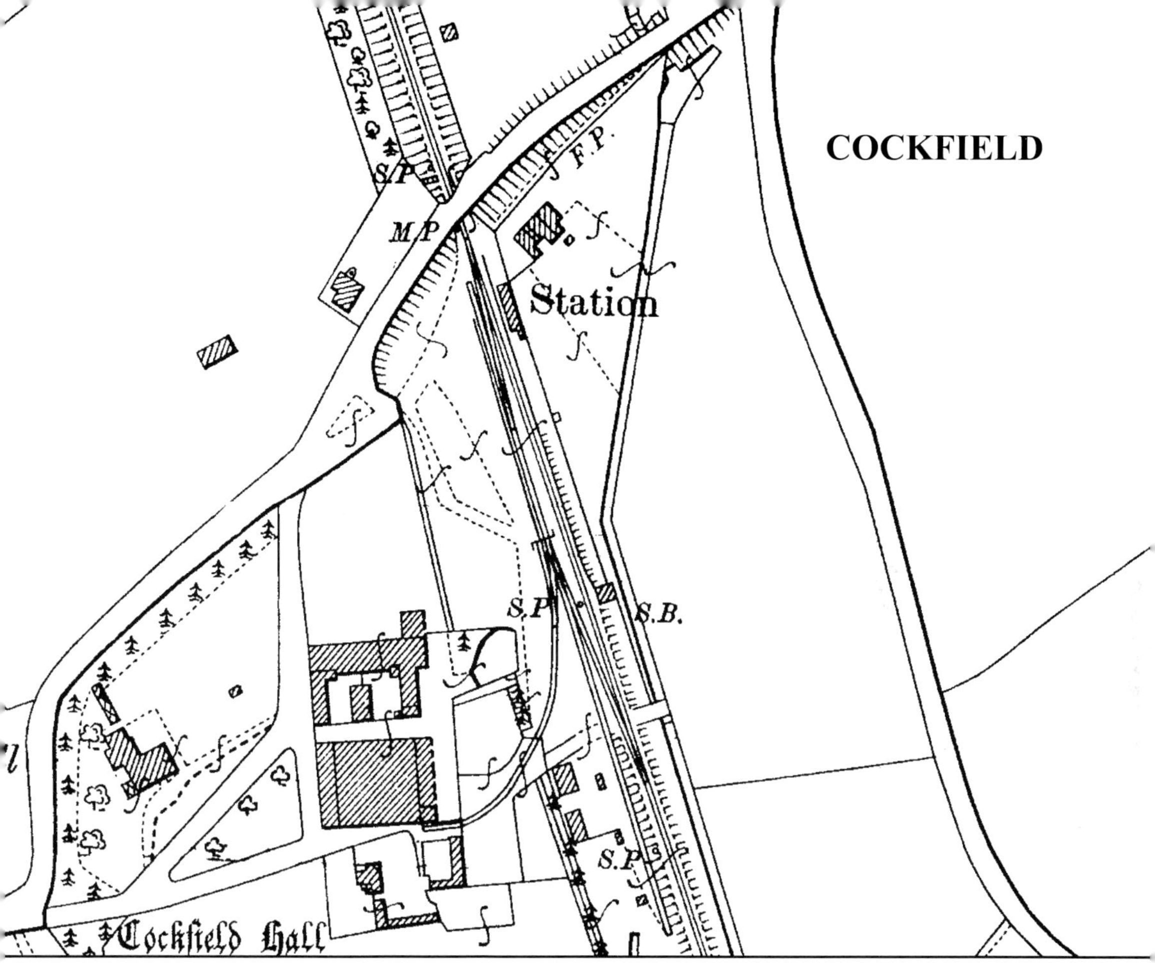

XVI. The suffix (SUFFOLK) was in use from 1st October 1927 until 9th September 1951. The 1904 survey shows that the road had been diverted northwards when the bridge was built. The private siding was for D.Hodge & Sons, at that time.

86. It appears that access to the platform was over the line behind the full wagon. No wonder loading gauges were required. The station was late opening, it coming into use on 14th November 1870. (P.Laming coll.)

87. The crane on the dock was rated at 30cwt. The signal box had 18 levers and was usable until 14th October 1962. It was not possible to pass trains here. There were 854 residents in the nearby village in 1901. (P.Laming coll.)

6454
GREAT EASTERN RAILWAY
Issued subject to Regulations in the Company's Time Tables.
BURY EAST GATE to
Bury East Gate Bury East Gate
COCKFIELD
Cockfield Cockfield
7d. Fare 7d.
THIRD CLASS
6454

0852
GREAT EASTERN RAILWAY
Issued subject to Regulations in the Company's Time Tables.
BURY EAST GATE to
Bury East Gate Bury East Gate
CHAPPEL
Chappel Chappel
Third Class
0852

88. The benefits of cats whiskers are evident as a DMU rolls in on 8th April 1961. Road vehicles used the crossing backwards when parcel traffic was to be moved. The main buildings were still standing 50 years later. (B.Pask)

89. Goods traffic continued until 19th April 1965, two months before this record of a Morris Minor was made from the road bridge. Cockfield made history when its urinal was removed to the EARM for posterity. (R.M.Casserley)

LAVENHAM

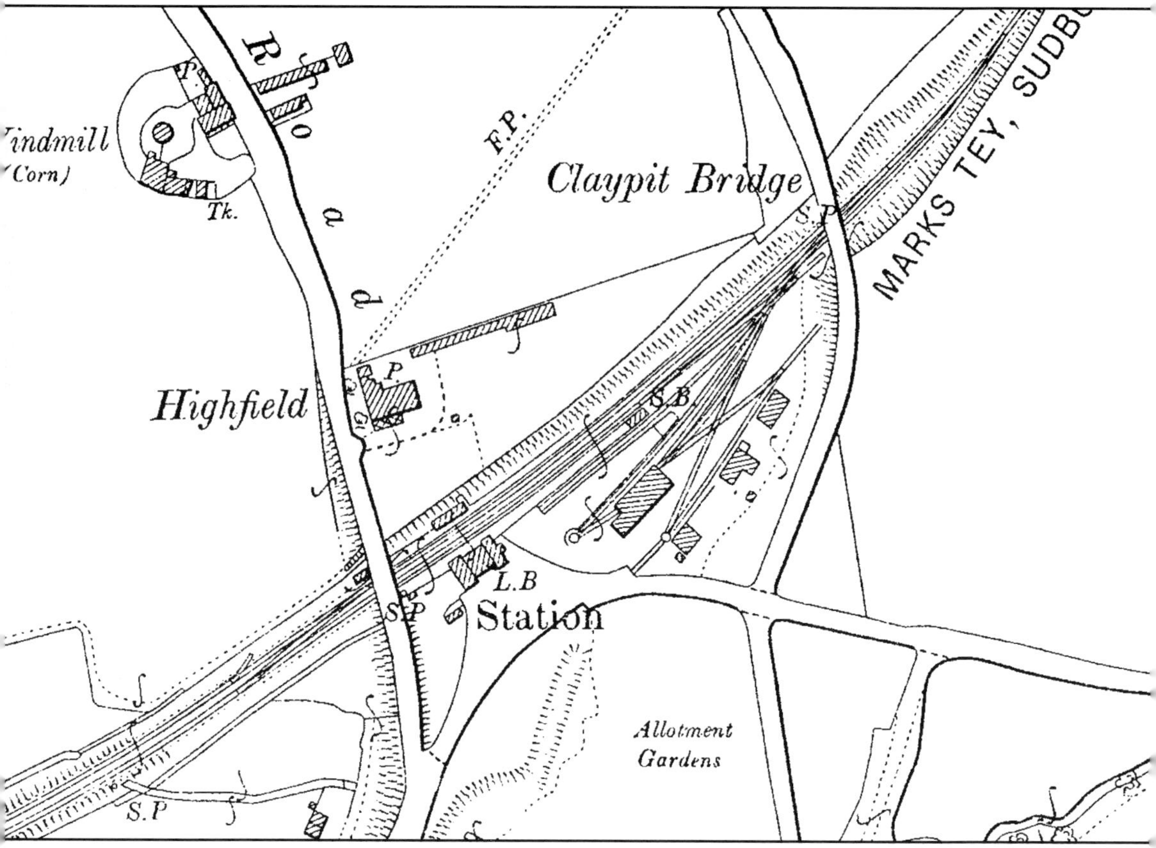

XVII. The 1904 survey indicates that a congested layout was inevitable, with two roads so close. At least the station could be easily reached from either one. The location was noted for textile production.

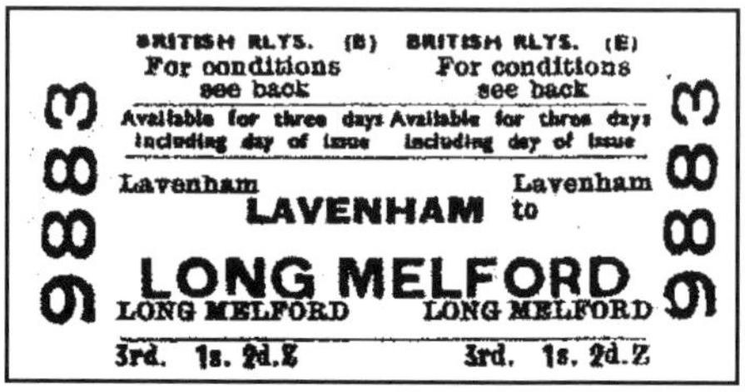

90. This view is from the bridge on the right of the map and has the goods shed centre stage. On the left is a haystack, probably produced from lineside vegetation and ready for fuelling the company's cart horses. There was a 22cwt crane in the goods shed. (P.Laming coll.)

91. The southeast facade has the house for the station master on the left and the booking hall centre. The Royal Mail letterbox is at the right end of the sheltered area. (P.Laming coll.)

92. Class J15 0-6-0 no. 65475 comes in with a train bound for Sudbury in about 1959. The signal box had 26 levers and was operational until 14th October 1962. (G.H.Hunt/Colour-Rail.com)

93. It is 4th June 1961 and the last train to traverse the route was recorded. The line was closed totally south hereof after that time. The population was only 1305; it had been 2018 in 1901. (B.Pask)

94. The same train is seen again, with no. D5537 in charge. The crossing had to be used by both staff and passengers to reach the platform on the left. (B.Pask)

95. This photograph was taken shortly after closure to passengers and just before the signs were removed. The goods yard remained in use until 19th April 1965. An industrial estate now occupies the site. (Lens of Sutton coll.)

LONG MELFORD

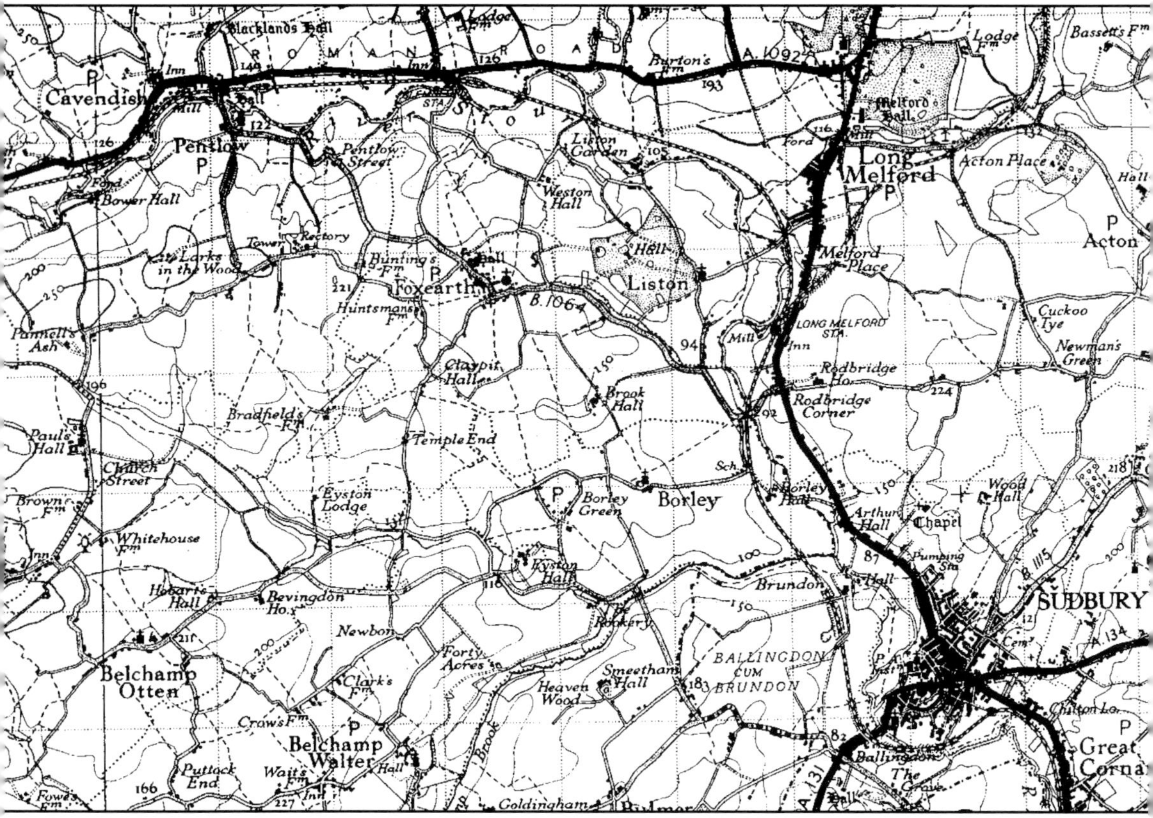

XVIII. The 1946 survey at 1ins to 1 mile has our route from Bury St. Edmunds top right and the one from Haverhill on the left. The circuitous route around Sudbury is explained later.

96. Carriages await the wealthy; the north end of the village was a mile away. It housed 3253 in 1901 and 2416 in 1961. (P.Laming coll.)

XIX. The 1927 edition at 20ins to 1 mile includes a turntable for use by locomotives of trains terminating. The nearby signal box was in use from 1889 until 1912. Yard Box was then built close by and its 26-lever frame functioned until 18th February 1934. The right line at the bottom is a long siding or headshunt.

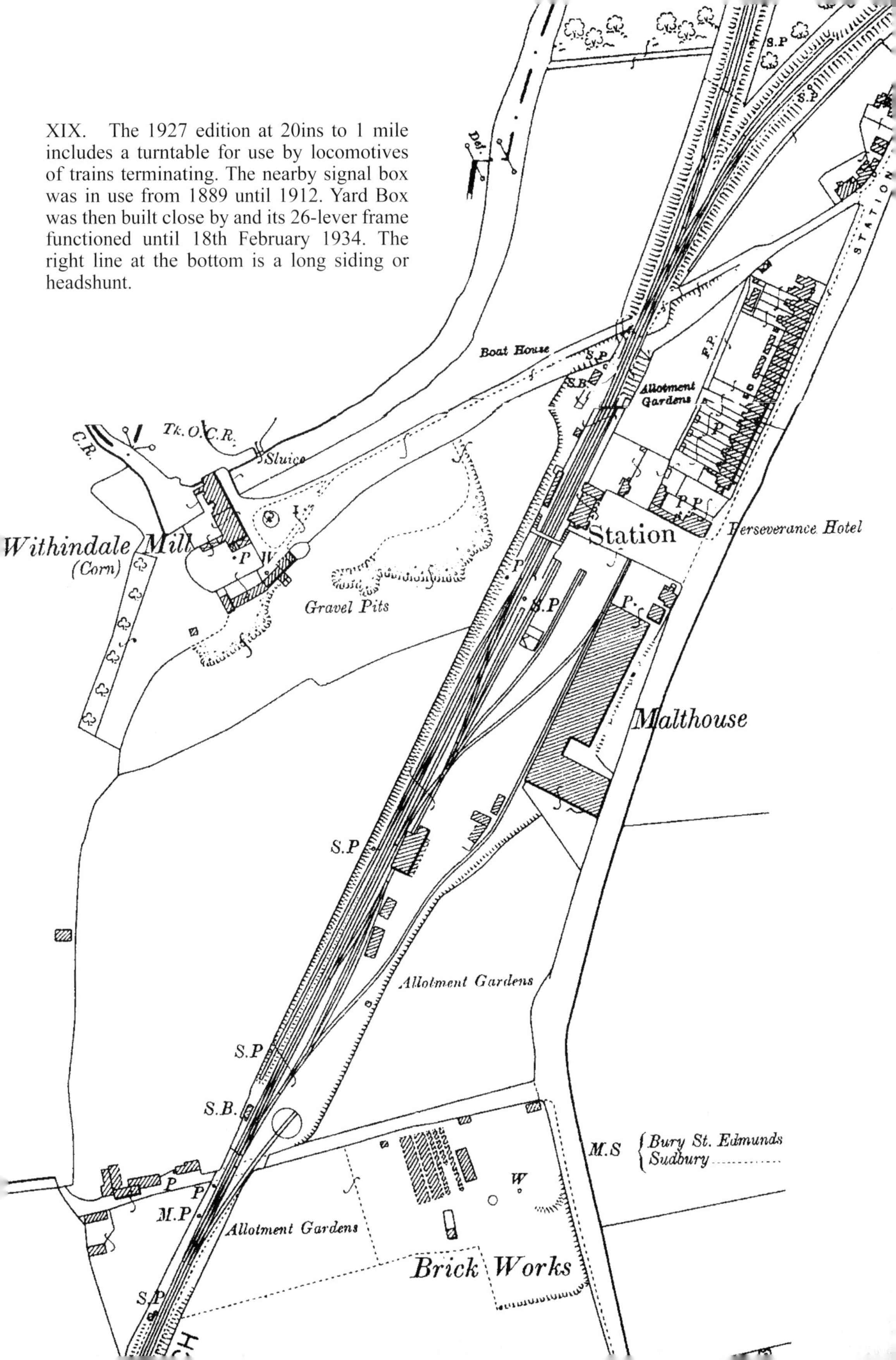

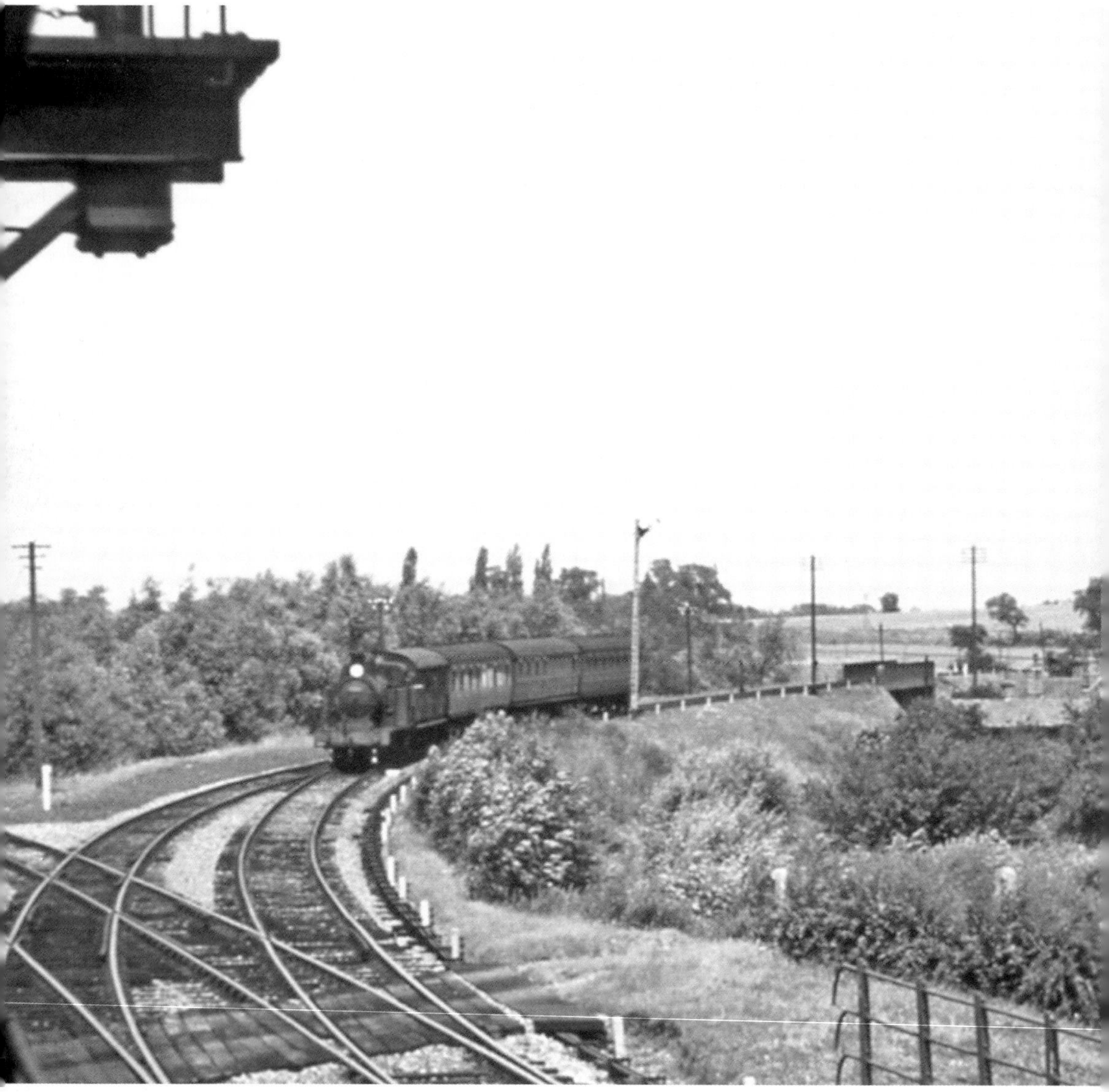

97. The skew bridge over the A134 is on the right in this view north from the signal box. Class E4 2-4-0 no. 62793 is running in from Bury St. Edmunds, but the date is not known. (Colour-Rail.com)

98. A train for Bury St. Edmunds awaits the connection from the south, which is already signalled for Haverhill. The massive wall on the right assures the security of gentlemen. (R.F.Roberts/SLS coll.)

99. The down side included the water tank and Junction Box. A 2-4-0 stands on the staff crossing, as a lad is deep in thought, probably longing for a cab ride. LONG was added as a prefix on 1st February 1884. (Dr. I.C.Scotchman coll.)

100. A postman with a mailbag waits for 2-4-0 no. 62785 to stop on 19th September 1952. There was a refreshment room here for many years. There could be a long wait between trains. (D.C.Pearce)

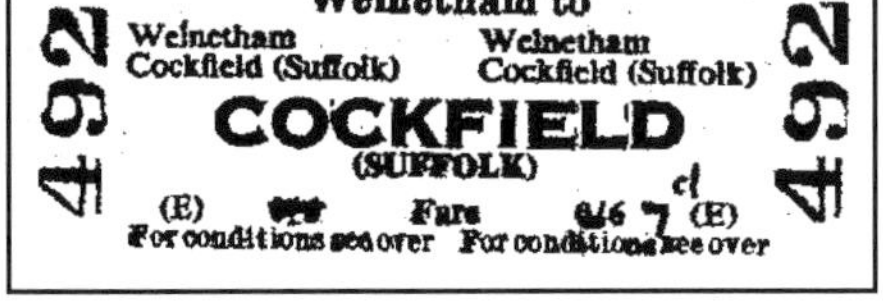

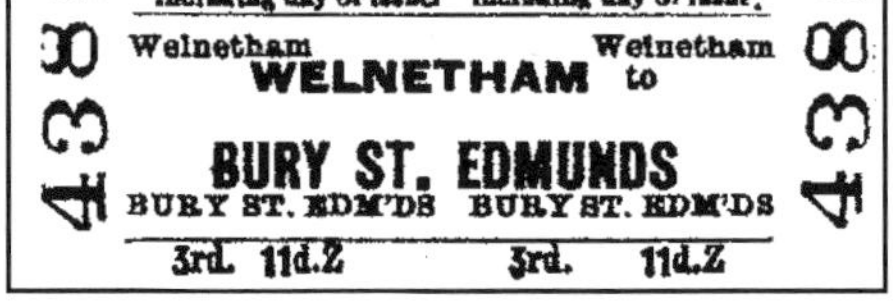

101. Class E4 no. 62790 is on the right and is working from Cambridge to Colchester on 13th October 1955. Waiting on the left is class J15 0-6-0 no. 65391, having terminated the 2.8pm from Bury St. Edmunds. (R.F.Roberts/SLS coll.)

102. Another J15, this time no. 65477, runs in from the south with a train destined for Bury St. Edmunds on 22nd May 1959. The maltings on the left became flats and the station building was adapted as a house. (J.Langford)

103. Built in 1912, Junction Box was in use until 6th March 1967. Its frame was enlarged from 35 to 45 levers in 1934, when Yard Box closed. (Lens of Sutton coll.)

104. The end is nigh as another DMU enters from the north and the signalman waits to collect the tablet from the driver. The goods yard closed on 12th September 1966. (Dr G.B.Sutton)

4. Sudbury

SUDBURY (SUFFOLK)

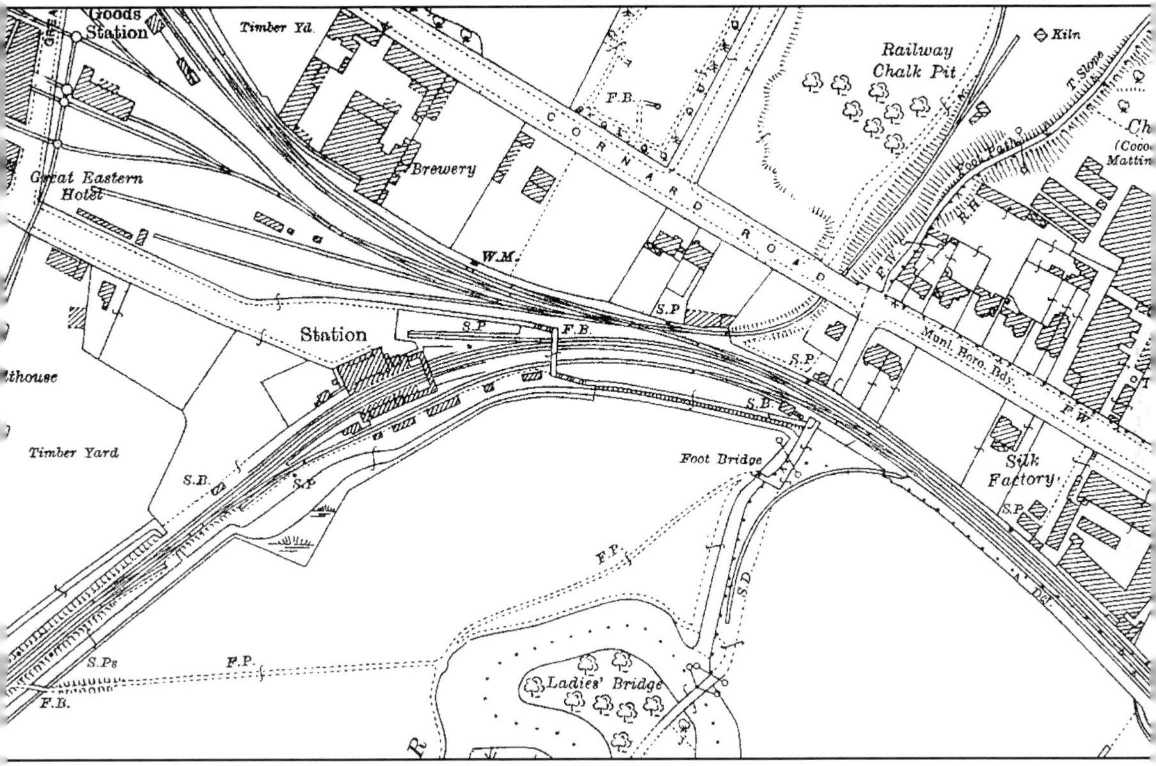

XX. The first station was a terminal one and was top left on this 1926 map at 20ins to 1 mile. It was in use as such from 1849 until 1865, when the curved line opened with a new station on it. This ran round the south of the town, as shown on map XVIII. The suffix has been in regular use since 1932, as the name is duplicated in northwest London.

105. This is the 1865 station long after its opening, judging by the ivy. It is the north elevation and the entrance to the goods wharf is on the left. (P.Laming coll.)

106. The facilities came into use on 9th August 1865 and are seen in good order in LNER days. The sign will have its standard dark blue background. (Dr I.C.Scotchman coll.)

Extract from Bradshaw's Guide for 1866. (Reprinted by Middleton Press 2011)

SUDBURY.

POPULATION, 6,879.

A telegraph station.

HOTEL.—Rose and Crown.

COACHES to and from Melford, daily.

MARKET DAY.—Saturday.

FAIRS.—March 12th, July 10th, and Dec. 12th, for earthenware.

SUDBURY is a market town and borough, in the county of Suffolk, situated on the north-eastern side of the river Stour, over which there is a bridge. Formerly it was a place of much greater importance than at present. It was one of the first places at which Edward III. settled the Flemings, whom he invited to England to instruct his subjects in the woollen manufacture. This business accordingly flourished here for some centuries, but the trade has long since declined. *St. Gregory's Church* was built by Archbishop Simon de Sudbury (a native), who was murdered here by Wat Tyler's mob, and buried near the college, the gate of which remains. Gainsborough, the painter, and Enfield, author of the "Speaker," &c., were natives.

107. The old terminal platforms and buildings are seen in the goods yard on 15th April 1949. The engines are nos 62788 and E2794. Between them is their source of coal. The engine shed is on the right and the stables are beyond the left locomotive. The shed was soon to be demolished and then engines were serviced in the open. The code was Sub to 31A and there were three locomotives based here in the 1930s. (W.A.Camwell/SLS coll.)

108. Departing on 7th July 1956 is class J15 no. 65390 with the 1.26pm Cambridge to Colchester. The signalman of Sudbury Goods is passing the tablet hoop to the crew. The 1889 box had 35 levers when closed on 15th February 1981. (R.M.Casserley)

B2

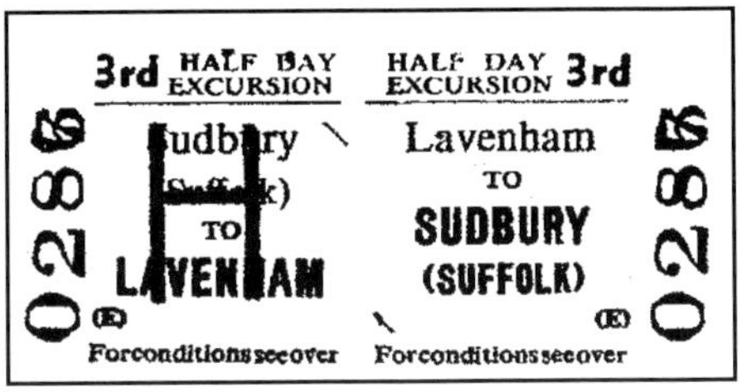

← 109. A class 105 DMU has the starting signal off and its tail lamp in place ready for its trip south, sometime in the 1960s. Cats whiskers lasted only a few years. (Lens of Sutton coll.)

110. The goods wharf and siding are seen from the public footbridge on 8th February 1960. The public footpath is on the far side of the wharf. Class J17 0-6-0 no. 65520 is on shunting duty. (Colour-Rail com.)

111. No. D5537 is northbound on 4th June 1961, returning the train seen in pictures 93 and 94. The other end of the loop on the right can be seen on the right of the next photograph. (B.Pask)

112. The public footbridge is viewed from the station footbridge on 27th June 1965, as a Derby Lightweight DMU arrives, bound for Cambridge. The barrow crossing is in the foreground. (Colour-Rail.com)

113. The line to the goods yard is on the left, the running lines are centre and the loop is on the right. Station Box had been at the other end of it until 1934; it had opened in 1889 with 19 levers. (B.Pask)

114. Parts of both footbridges are evident in this eastward view from February 1967. The extent of the check rails differs on the running lines. Staffing had ceased on 15th August 1966. (R.F.Roberts/SLS coll.)

← 115. Retaining their cats whiskers are two DMUs resting in the good yard. This is the location of picture 107. The cattle dock was to the right of the camera. (Lens of Sutton coll.)

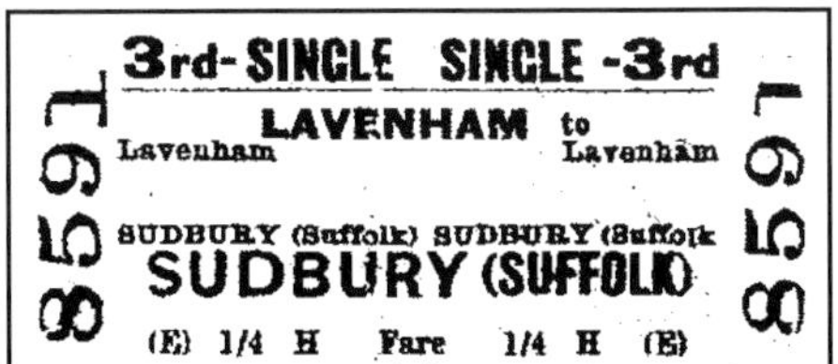

116. The footbridge was moved and is in use at the EARM. The entire loop is seen at last, as is the wharf siding, also the barrow crossing. Note the perforated concrete signal post, seen on 5th May 1967. (B.Pask)

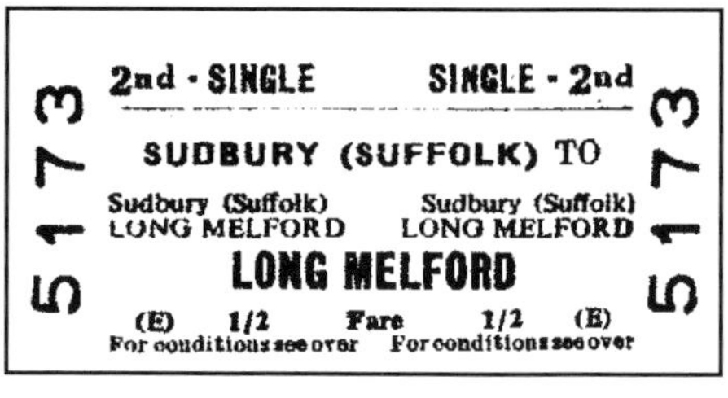

117. The goods yard was recorded on the same day, but it had closed on 31st October 1966. On the right is the brewery building. This was a valuable town centre site, awaiting development. (B.Pask)

118. Buildings had crept across the trackbed, but the station still stood in 1988. It was used as a museum for a short period, but the vandals won. Litter abounds, how sad. (Milepost 92½)

119. All was not lost, as a new two-coach platform was built on the original terminal route alignment and it is seen on 12th January 1991. It had opened on 28th October 1990 and soon was carrying increasing traffic. (Dr I.C.Scotchman)

120. An unusual visitor was the NENTA charter from Newcastle on 15th July 2006, with no. 31128 nearest and no. 47703 on the other end. The station had its best service ever and all rejoiced that the fight had been worthwhile. (Dr I.C.Scotchman)